D1589079

RESULT

THINK DECISIVELY, TAKE ACTION AND GET RESULTS

Phil Olley

PEARSON

Harlow, England • London • New York • Boston • San Francisco • Toronto • Sydney
Auckland • Singapore • Hong Kong • Tokyo • Seoul • Taipei • New Delhi
Cape Town • São Paulo • Mexico City • Madrid • Amsterdam • Munich • Paris • Milan

To Dad

PEARSON EDUCATION LIMITED

Edinburgh Gate
Harlow CM20 2JE
Tel: +44 (0)1279 623623
Fax: +44 (0)1279 431059
Website: www.pearson.com/uk

First published in Great Britain in 2013 (print and electronic)

© Phil Olley Consulting 2013 (print and electronic)

Pearson Education is not responsible for the content of third-party internet sites.

ISBN: 978-0-273-77948-3 (print)
 978-0-273-78160-8 (ePub)
 978-0-273-78161-5 (PDF)

British Library Cataloguing-in-Publication Data
A catalogue record for this book is available from the British Library

Library of Congress Cataloging-in-Publication Data
A catalog record for this book is available from the Library of Congress

10 9 8 7 6 5 4 3 2 1
17 16 15 14 13

Cartoons by Bill Piggins
Cover design by Dan Mogford
Typeset in 11pt Helevetica Neue Light by 30
Printed in Great Britain by Henry Ling Ltd, Dorchester, Dorset

NOTE THAT ANY PAGE CROSS REFERENCES REFER TO THE PRINT EDITION

Contents

CHAPTER 5 GOAL SETTING → GOAL GETTING 55

Forget SMART and stepping out of comfort zones. This is how high achievers set goals.

PART II GET SET – Ready to move in the right direction 79

CHAPTER 6 THE MASTER PLAN 81

Planning is about creating a strategy, not a straightjacket. An outline plan of how you are going to reach your result.

CHAPTER 7 GENERATIVE THINKING 93

A toolkit to help you think creatively, and decisively, so that thinking leads to results.

CHAPTER 8 AWESOME SPECIAL MISSIONS (ASMs) 105

The short-term 'project goals' that help you make breakthroughs and move up your strategic mountain quickly. Here's how to set them, and create huge energy and fast action.

CHAPTER 9 Motiv-ACTION 121

What, specifically, will make you do it?

PART III GO! – Action is the key 131

CHAPTER 10 FOCUSED ACTION 133

How to take breakthrough action, to build persistence and ensure maximum productivity at all times.

CHAPTER 16 HAVING A SELF-UPGRADE 227

Everyone has a set of beliefs about what will make them successful. The way you look, the way you act, the words you use, the way you think all have a bearing on the results you achieve. Time for an upgrade.

CHAPTER 17 KEEPING ON TRACK 243

How to self-coach to success, so that you can stay on track. How to avoid being deflected by fear; and how to maintain the right attitude, courage and commitment to achieve your goals.

CHAPTER 18 BUILDING BRILLIANT HABITS 257

How to build great habits that support you – a 28-day programme.

CHAPTER 19 YOUR ACTION PLAN 265

Use every principle, every tool in the book in a step-by-step plan.

About the author

Following an exciting military career, **PHIL OLLEY** entered business in 1990. From his subsequent wide experience of sales and business, he began to distil the ingredients of success into clearly understandable principles and, following a life-threatening (and life-changing) near death experience, he established Phil Olley Consulting in 1999, quickly  becoming a sought-after inspirational coach and presenter.

Phil has written many articles and columns for business magazines, been featured in the national press, writes a regular column for *The Market* magazine, and has appeared on BBC radio and prime-time TV programmes.

His first book, *Counting Chickens – The 'Nexus' principles for personal and professional development*, first published in 2003, and reprinted in 2011, has already 'gone international', a second edition being specially produced for an Asian audience.

He was one of a select group of speakers chosen to address the Business Startup Show at London's prestigious ExCel Conference Centre, attended by over 15,000 people.

In addition to speaking at conferences and business events, and running masterclasses and seminars, he works with select individual clients on a one-to-one basis: in both the UK, and throughout the rest of the world; from Europe to the USA; and to the Far East.

His performance-coaching methods and processes have been adopted in programmes with many commercial organisations and with UNICEF and The World Food Programme.

He is founder and broadcaster of The FOCUS Gym, a truly unique programme – available worldwide as a daily seven-minute conference service helping individuals from all professions, all walks of life, to achieve outstanding personal results.

www.philolley.com

Acknowledgements

To all those I've worked with and coached, individually, as teams, or in larger groups – I am always learning from you!

To my editor, Elie Williams, who has challenged and ensured clarity of thought throughout, and been remarkably patient! And to the publishers, for taking it on.

Introduction

Let's consider this question: If you had a magic wand for your career, your business, your success, what would you wish for?

You see, when you consider this, you probably get a fleeting glimpse crossing your mind of what really is possible, an inner vision of the results you genuinely would love to achieve. Now, imagine you have only one chance to get it right...

One chance to achieve that glittering career, that brilliant business, that specific achievement, that personal victory. If you had just one chance, you'd leave no stone unturned, right? And that's what this book is going to help you with. It's not about just 'being more motivated', or feeling a little better about life. It's about turning over all those stones and propelling yourself towards tangible, sustainable and continuous success.

Now, hold that thought.

You see, over many years of working with people who are successful, observing what they do to get results, and helping people reach greater heights, it has become apparent that successful people use the same set of simple principles, consciously or otherwise.

I observed that, for the high achievers, it's not things like SMART goals or stepping out of comfort zones that make the difference. It's far more powerful than that. And yet it's so often overlooked.

Think back to a time when you achieved a goal, a result, however great or small. Perhaps even as a child. You had the goal in mind, it became the centre of your attention, the most important point of focus of your life. You were enthused by it, had pure passion, focus and attention for it. That adrenalin was compelling and made you take action. I'll bet that, to this day, you look back on it with pride and a genuine feeling of satisfaction.

This moment already will have given you insight into what it takes to achieve results. This book will take those insights further, it will look at the things that push you forward to achieve your goals, and how you demolish the barriers that get in the way.

Because, everyone has the capability to achieve results, and the capacity for success. Everyone can reach a goal. You probably already know, deep down, what you can do to reach new levels of achievement. This book is about helping you to overcome the barriers, and unleash your automatic result-achieving ability.

It's one thing to read the book and understand the principles, but to really make the ideas work you need to apply them constantly and consistently, moment-by-moment, day-by-day, week-by-week, month-by-month – as a habit. To help you I have focused on the practical applications that you will be able to implement immediately.

H-O-W TO GET THE MOST FROM THIS BOOK

Honesty

Open-mindedness

Willingness to act

Firstly, you will need to be **H**onest with yourself. Many people, when faced with a 'common sense' idea for achieving better results, think to themselves, 'Oh yeah, well I do that already.' In fact, because it appears to be common sense, they just *imagine* that they do it already. This book is about turning common sense into common practice.

Secondly, you will need **O**pen-mindedness. This is crucial in creating results. It's no good holding on to those attitudes and ideas that may be holding you back.

And, thirdly, you will need **W**illingness to take action. Just reading this book will change very little. This is not an academic exercise. We're going to cover some specific actions to take – none of which are, in themselves, very difficult, but they do require action.

Enthusi-ACTION

People often get buzzed up when reading a book on professional development and success. So enthusiastic, in fact, that they can't wait to tell others of the new insights.

And that's when the trouble starts!

You see, when we say things like, 'I'm reading a great book about x, and I'm now going to do z', the initial reaction is sometimes one of scepticism, even from our greatest supporters. That psychological interference received from someone else, even as a mere glance, or raised eye-brow, can be enough to derail you.

So, can I suggest a ground-rule? Don't tell anyone else (no matter how close they are) that you are reading this book.

First, read it, take action, and then allow others to notice the changes it makes to you. Let them be persuaded by the fact that you are achieving new results. Then you can tell them and suggest they might like to buy their own copy – available at all good bookstores and ereaders!

Your Enthusi-ACTION is far more valuable to you, and a greater persuader to others, than mere enthusiasm.

'STRATAGRAMS' AND Visual-is-ACTION TECHNIQUES

Throughout, I have included a number of strategic diagrams ('Stratagrams') to explain the concepts and practical tools and to help you experience the thought processes to translate goals into action.

The visualisation (aka Visual-is-ACTION) techniques are also a key component. You will know exactly what I mean when we come to them. Whilst there will be no quick fixes, in using the Visual-is-ACTION tools you will notice some specific changes very quickly – normally within the first 28 days.

There's another factor, too. Now, I don't know fully how an aeroplane works. But I still get on them, along with many other people. And none of us asks the captain or airline owner to give a full run down on how the aircraft is going to fly before we get aboard.

You see, it always amazes me the way people approach improving their results – very often they are unwilling to believe the very ideas that will create the result. Even though they need something new, they carry on with the things that aren't working for them. Often people approach any changes in an ad-hoc, piecemeal fashion, and many simply settle with a little tip, or a small improvement here or there, or a little 'self-help'. But, this approach rarely makes a real change.

You are different. You don't have to settle for mere increments, or minor improvements. You can start a personal revolution. And this starts by embracing a new approach to achieving results – becoming a result-aholic!

If some of the ideas, concepts, tools and techniques in this book initially feel uncomfortable, don't worry. Have faith. In fact, it's very likely that the techniques you initially feel most uncomfortable about will provide you with the greatest breakthroughs.

TIME FOR FOCUS

Isn't it amazing how moment-by-moment, so very few people are truly focused? You know, really *here* – grounded, and concentrating on this moment and the result at hand.

Are you opening this book for the first time, partly distracted by a whole host of external clutter? Are you ready to focus on the content and take some action as a result, or would it be better to save it and come back later when you are able to devote the right focus to it?

You see, what I've discovered about those who are most successful in any walk of life is that they commit whole-heartedly to whatever they take on. That's how they get results. So, let's adopt that mindset, and go for full-on commitment. Take notes, put red asterisks at key parts; highlight and underline to your heart's content. And, when required, get into the Action Zones.

This is for those who genuinely want to make a breakthrough and achieve new results. The only qualifying factor is that you are serious about making the changes you really do desire.

OK. Now, ready?

Then, let's get started.

PART I

On Your Marks
The fundamentals of getting results

There are certain perspectives and character traits that all successful high achievers display and that you must develop to improve your results.

CHAPTER 1

What's Stopping You?

3 per cent of people make things happen
10 per cent of people have things happen to them
87 per cent of people haven't a clue what's happening!

Results are unavoidable. Everything you do gets a result.

In fact, everything you are and everything you have, is a result.

The key is to be getting the results *we want* in order to take us to the success we want.

A SLICE OF PERSONAL PHIL-OSOPHY – THE GIFT

The greatest gift I ever received occurred on 18 March 1999. Here's how it unfolded.

I was a normally healthy, mid-thirties, average type of guy. On three occasions that early spring I had come out in an unexplained rash from head to toe. Like an allergic reaction. The fourth instance was to have almost tragic consequences.

I was in Edinburgh with my wife, Elizabeth, when it began, and it began just as it had done on the previous occasions, with a tingling heat sensation on the back of my head, spreading to my ears and, from my hands, spreading up my arms and, from my belly, spreading to my chest, waistline and the rest of my body.

Time to get back to the car to drive home. By the time we reached the car, the rash had become a puffiness and my face had begun to swell. I slumped into the passenger seat. I could literally see the nerve endings in my eyeballs as I went snow-blind, like a white cloud. The nauseating taste in my mouth told me I was going to pass out.

But I wasn't passing out. I was passing away.

At the moment my body slumped forward, my tongue swelled to fill my mouth, my mind went into overdrive. I felt myself stop breathing, and I knew for a split second that this was it. This must be how it ends.

As I floated down the white tunnel, I was shrouded in an eerie silence – a unique soundlessness.

When they say your life flashes before you, that's not true. It's your *values* that flash before you. And it was my *values* that flashed before me – in my final instant.

And, along with that, the regrets of what I hadn't done with my life.

What about the things I hadn't seen, done, achieved yet?

What about all the things left undone?

> **One day your life will flash before your eyes. Make sure it's worth seeing**

I woke up on the pavement (I subsequently learned that it was several minutes later), surrounded by paramedics, with my body constrained on a stretcher, and a mask being forced to my face.

What happened? A car crash?

'No, mate... an anaphylactic shock they call it. You died. And now you are alive.'

It was later explained that my body had simply shut down like a computer shuts down. And, eventually, my vital functions had stopped.

Since then, after numerous tests, no hint has been found as to the cause, or the trigger, for the reaction.

They called it an anaphylactic shock. I call it a gift. I am lucky. I had a Near-Death Experience. Too many people end their days having had a Near-Life Experience.

SUCCESS

When I first meet potential clients they often tell me they feel like they are stuck in treacle, and not really genuinely getting anywhere – whether in their business or career, or their life in general. They feel in a bit of a quagmire.

Business owners tell me that the reason they started out in business was to have more freedom and control, and yet these things are the first two things that are sacrificed on the altar of running their own business. Their business is running them.

For many people, even if they start to make changes, sustaining them becomes almost impossible. The result is that they go back to where they were – perhaps even feeling it's one step forward two steps back or, even if they are a little bit better off, they certainly haven't waved a magic wand and achieved anything dramatically different.

You know, it doesn't have to be like that. It's time to make some changes.

One of the main reasons people never get out of the quagmire, out of the life treacle, is that they haven't specifically decided on what the alternative is, what success is for them. You see, knowing what success is for us, provides the context for deciding the results we want to achieve. It makes us purposeful – literally.

Now, I don't intend to get bogged down in definitions of 'success' – greater minds than mine have wrestled with it for centuries and will, no doubt, continue to do so. It will suffice simply to open up the question, and provide some guidelines so you can create your own answers.

Let's get two things absolutely straight:

1 Success is different things to different people

Whatever your version of success, it's *your* version, based on what's important to you – your values. And your version is perfectly valid.

2 Success is fun

Too many people focus on the hassle they *perceive* will surround them in becoming 'successful'. It sounds just like a load of hard work, and extra stuff to do on top of an already busy schedule. It is intrinsically associated with extra discipline.

However, whatever your definition of success is, I would be so bold as to suggest that, if it's not fun, it's not success.

Yes, some 'sacrifices' will be made along the way, but these are not really sacrifices. They aren't even 'paying the price'. They are '*investments in success*'.

The top sportspeople *invest* training time and pounding the roads when others don't. The world-class concert pianist *invests* several hours every day at the piano, when others don't. The top business-people *invest* their time, energy, money to create the results they want and others just don't.

BOILING FROGS AND WHINING DOGS

Many years ago in his book, *The Age of Unreason*, Charles Handy used the analogy of what happens when you place a frog in a pan of water and gently heat the pan. The water heats up, and the frog is boiled to death before it notices a change in temperature. It simply didn't recognise the change in external environment and do anything about it.

We are currently in danger of sitting in boiling water ourselves as the world around us faces the most fundamental changes since the industrial revolution. Politically, economically, sociologically and technologically this is an unrivalled period of change. Many people have misunderstood it as some sort of recession. It's not. It's not a dip, double or otherwise. It's a new world order.

There's only one way to thrive in this new world order, and that's by having a personal revolution. Not evolution, revolution. A decisive change in approach, a genuine transformation in achievement – not just incrementally getting a little better, but nothing short of a complete breakthrough.

The story of the Whining Dog is an old Chinese tale:

A dog was sitting on a chair at the porch, whining away. Another dog came by, heard the distress, stopped and asked, 'Hey, what's the matter?'

'I am sitting on a nail,' came the reply.

'So why don't you move?'

'Oh, it isn't hurting enough', groaned the whining dog!

And, in the current climate, if you sit still... Well, I'm sure you get the picture.

What has become apparent to me is that, fundamentally,

Success is CHOSEN

That's right. You choose success. Or not. Isn't that great news? You choose.

And this choice takes place at a range of levels, from the small, almost unconscious, actions and decisions you take every moment of every day, up to the big strategic decisions and actions you take with your life.

SO, WHAT'S STOPPING YOU?

There are, in fact, nine main reasons people don't make breakthroughs and achieve the results they want in life:

1 Lack of purpose/vision – an inability to see that big picture.

2 Lack of specific goals and objectives.

3 Lack of knowledge or know-how.

4 Lack of order and organisation.

5 Old beliefs, attitudes and a poor mindset.

6 Failure to distinguish priorities and allocate resources appropriately.

7 Fear – of failure, rejection, loss (risk), or even fear of success itself.

8 Low self-esteem and lack of confidence.

9 Resistance to change.

All of these lead to a tendency for people to get stuck and stay as they are. Most people limit themselves, allowing the blockers to triumph. Successful people are faced with the same challenges, the same apparent limitations as everyone, yet they have a habit of breaking through those blockers.

Perhaps now is the moment to *choose success*.

The results you have got so far in life are the consequence of your choices, not necessarily conscious choices, but choices all the same. The quality of our lives always rests with the choices we make.

Not choosing is also a choice. This is both your one chance, and your one choice. *Not choosing* is *choosing not* to change.

If your life depended on it, could you choose to change? Yes!

Well, here's the news: your life does depend on it! The quality of your results rests with your choice now – to change.

> *Definition of insanity:*
> *continuing to do the same things and*
> *expecting different results*

Whilst there are an infinite variety of answers to the question 'What is success?', all the routes to 'success' have common themes, shared principles in action. And making the breakthrough to change is at the core.

To make any change, first, the **S**uccess (or required outcome) needs to be identified.

Then the **R**esult (or series of results) needed to reach that success is quantified.

From this a set of new or improved **A**ctions can be determined which will lead to those results.

If the actions are habits, the new results will be consistent and the success will be sustained. If the actions are not developed into habits, the results will be short-lived and the success will not be sustained. Which is why **M**indset is so important.

The MARS Formula

Mindset

Action

Result

Success

People always default to habits and, for these actions to become habits, it is the mindset that allows them to become automatic and consistent.

Which is where we are heading next.

But first…

1 **Decision time**. So, now you are ready to change.

   Just make the decision, and write on a card:

   'I have made the decision to change'.

   And remember this moment forever.

   Take a few seconds to celebrate that change. How exciting it is to have decided to change, to be making the change, to be choosing success.

2 **Change something in the next 24 hours**. It is important at this stage to do something different to signify the change. It's not just about thinking 'things are changing' or 'I'm going to change'. It's about making the changes for yourself. So, within the next 24 hours, change something – just for the act of making a change.

Maybe you just decide to go to the gym, to get up earlier, to make more sales calls, or do something to move your business into a new league, to do whatever feels right for you – a change you know deep down is going to have a positive impact.

Just do it, and enjoy the fact that you have made a change.

Chapter key points

- Results are all around – they are unavoidable. Everything we do gets a result. The key is to get the results you choose.

- We are in a time of great change, heralding a New World Order. Many people get stuck in a quagmire of being too busy to make changes, to achieve results. It's time to choose your success, and the results you want to achieve that success. This requires a definite decision to change.

- There are nine reasons people don't achieve their true potential, and everyone faces these 'blockers'. Successful people simply find ways, consciously and unconsciously, of overcoming these barriers.

- Mindset is crucial for sustaining action changes that lead to new results, as we'll see…

Action Zone

Time to download

My 'What's Stopping You?' Action Zone

What I have learned	What I am going to do about it

CHAPTER 2

The Achiever's Mindset

'If you can dream it, you can do it.' WALT DISNEY

What is it that generates focus, and ensures you achieve results?

What is the magic ingredient that leads to success? Is it just luck? Right time, right place? After the fact, it often appears that way.

What are the 3 per cent of people 'at the top' really doing?

What's the real 'secret'?

Well, it's not what you may think.

You see, success and achievement are our natural state. The natural human trait is unique excellence and brilliance. But the trend is towards the average, anonymous. Successful people all experience the same barriers as everyone else. It's the way they overcome those barriers, and the way they deploy their traits consistently, that makes the difference. The good news is: we all have these traits.

Those who do succeed embrace and access the natural ability of humans to be brilliant, breaking through the barriers that hold others at bay.

Many people talk about belief and desire being key components of reaching for success, and I would agree absolutely. *But*, most of them stop there, and you are simply left wondering how to apply these key components and, crucially, how to change and upgrade them. This chapter is about how our beliefs work and how we can change them.

BELIEF AND DESIRE

What do we mean by 'belief'? I mean, you believe the sun will come up tomorrow morning, right? Well, is that the same level of belief that you have to have in your goals? And desire, what does that really mean? You are probably thinking right now, well yes, I do desire success, I do *want* to be successful. So, what do we mean by 'desire'? And, most importantly, how can we harness our upgraded beliefs and desires to translate into actions that lead to success?

In those people who are most successful a substantial link exists between what they see and believe, and the swift and decisive actions they take and their ability to get results. And when observing what successful people do and listening to what they say, it became evident to me that they were

dispelling one of the greatest myths ever perpetrated –
'Don't count your chickens before they hatch!'

We get told this pearl of wisdom from an early age, usually
by the people we love and respect the most. They say it out
of love and protection for us. They mean no harm, of course.
And yet it creates a mindset of not being definite about our
goals, about what we believe can and will happen.

Successful people don't limit themselves in this way. They
have a knack of automatically 'counting their chickens' using
their mindset and heartset: their belief and desire. It's that
belief and desire that make it happen. The belief and desire
come first. Not just hoping and wishing for a result. It is
genuine belief and confident expectation.

And the good news is that the counting chickens mindset
can be developed.

We also all know the phrase: 'Seeing is believing'. When you
see something, you believe it. And we know that what you
can believe, you can achieve. We achieve up to the level
we believe to be possible. In life, business, our careers, in
everything we do, we achieve what we believe. To achieve
a goal, we must believe we can achieve the goal. To believe
we can achieve the goal, we must see it, in our mind's eye,
being achieved.

Seeing = Believing = Achieving

PUTTING YOUR MIND TO IT: CONSCIOUS AND SUBCONSCIOUS

The mindset dome versus the comfort zone

The phrase 'comfort zone' is now a household term and a familiar concept to most.

Sadly, I believe, it is a commonly unquestioned tenet of most 'skills' trainers and coaches to constantly bark on about getting people to step out of their comfort zones in order to make changes and achieve new successes.

Why do I say 'sadly'?

Well, if we get people to step out of their comfort zone, we are employing a discipline. If this discipline is not backed up by developing a new mindset, the necessary habit will not be formed and, in a short space of time, the individual will step back into the comfort zone.

This is even more likely to happen when the 'going gets tough'. People tend to run for cover when they aren't hitting the new heights they so badly wish for. And, worse still, the comfort zone will not only be unchanged in scale, it will also be reinforced by the new sense of guilt/failure.

A better representation might be to consider our mindset as a dome, as shown in the following figure.

Mindset Dome

We are standing at the centre of the dome and all of our self-imposed limitations, beliefs, attitudes, associations and paradigms create an overarching barrier – a mindset dome.

We can achieve only what is first created in our mind and so, in order to take new actions to improve results on a consistent basis, we need to first expand the mindset dome and then operate at the new 'outer limit'. We must allow ourselves to believe that our new performance is not only achievable, but is, in fact, already being achieved.

We must first picture ourselves operating in the 'stretch zone', which then sends the signal to our mindset that we are achieving new heights. This belief will allow our new set of behaviours to become habits because they don't seem uncomfortable, as they are consistent with the extent of our newly stretched mindset dome. We find ourselves accommodating new habits much more quickly.

So, rather than stepping out of the comfort zone, improvements in performance, results and success come from expanding the mindset dome. Change the beliefs and allow the results to catch up.

> *The mind once expanded can never regain its former shape*

The more you see an outcome you want, the more you will believe it, and the more chance you have of achieving it, and that belief becomes an unconscious compulsion to achieve. This generates action that generates results that lead to success.

The key is in seeing the vision as if it's real – as if it's genuinely happening. The mind cannot distinguish between the images that are real and those that are imagined. Once 'seen', the subconscious mind simply acts on the associations generated by the vision. And by vision, here, I'm not just talking about images, but also gut-feelings and other associations.

How often do people hear a song on the radio and say, 'Oh, yes, I love this film!' Yes, they have instantly picked up that the song is from a film they like, and the mind has instantly made that shortcut association. And how often do you hear a song and think it reminds you of that school dance you went to – you know, you can even smell her perfume, can't you?

The same happens when you watch a scary TV film. You see pictures that are designed to frighten you and, even though your conscious, logical mind is saying, 'But it's only a film', the subconscious mind overrides it, and you display all the traits and characteristics of someone who is genuinely afraid. Such scary TV pictures mean we feel genuinely scared, and our behaviours match those of someone experiencing genuine fear – our heart rate goes up, blood pressure rises, palms start to sweat, and so on.

We can deduce from this, that *the mind cannot distinguish between what's real and what's imagined.*

Hold that thought. It really is important.

YOUR THOUGHT-PRINT

The 'mind' is not just the brain – it's cellular. Each of us has a unique mindset dome, an individual thought-print.

Our mind operates on stimuli that come from every cell of our body, every thought, every word, every action, every feeling, every experience, every ounce of energy expended. All these things add to our mindset. It's the memory carried around in every muscle, it's the associations conjured up by every fibre of our existence. Our mindset is all-encompassing and all-pervading. That's why it controls what we do and what we get, at every level.

We carry this unique thought-print around with us. It is the default setting – our unconscious being, our subconscious mind. It can process billions of pieces of information in a second, through our senses. And what is important to us will determine which bits of information get filtered out and which bits get acted upon. The conscious mind can process only a fraction of the information, which is why it is our subconscious mind that is the driving force of our actions, results, success.

The furball of failure

You know when an animal has a furball stuck in its throat, normally a result of constantly licking their own fur. The poor creature is paralysed by coughing and spluttering in an attempt to expel this ball of hair and fur.

In a similar way, many people carry round a furball of failure in their mind – a sort of huge ball of interconnected past 'failures', and things they did badly or got wrong.

This impacts our thought-print, our own image of ourselves and, more importantly, it affects what we believe we can or can't do, and who we are/are not, and what our *proper place'* in the world is.

This can lead to self-sabotaging thoughts like: 'success is for other people', 'that's just my luck, that is!', 'I'll never get anywhere'. And, hey presto, you have a self-fulfilling prophecy and that's why most end up failing – they're simply too scared to succeed.

Furball of Failure

Well, it doesn't have to be that way. And, if you study successful people, you'll realise they have a completely different perspective. They don't see the past as a series of failures. If they are looking back at the past at all, they see it as a series of lessons and experiences all leading along the journey to success.

Exercise

So, let's cough up that furball of failure – starting right now.

List all the experiences in the past that you are carrying around as deemed 'failures'.

Once you have that full list, next to each item, write the lesson you learned, or how valuable the experience was because of the character skill you developed.

'Failure'	Lesson learned
1	
2	
3	
4	
5	
6	
7	
8	
9	
10	

You may find that many of them will go back to your early days. And part of this exercise is to enable you to see that you may still be carrying around the experience of failure from a child's perspective, which probably isn't a great deal of use to you now. So, just find the lesson or skill you gained from the experience and then give your adult self a break!

Now look at that right-hand column, I'm willing to bet that it has a list of very useful skills and learning points, which you may not have learned any other way. So these apparent 'failures' actually delivered more in terms of your personal development than many of your successes.

You can see many examples of the power of failure throughout history:

- Edison tried and failed many thousands of times before he came up with a working lightbulb.
- Fleming discovered penicillin only because he was untidy and left one of his culture samples to go mouldy.
- Dr Kellogg's corn flakes were the result of allowing some cooked wheat to go stale.

ON A ROLL, IN THE ZONE

It's also critically important to understand that we can all go into periods where we are operating our achiever's mindset. You know where you are on a roll, when seemingly everything you do turns to gold. These are times when we are *in the zone*, as an athlete would say, engrossed, focused. Similarly, the opposite can be true.

This is a result of the mental state we are in. Most people just go with the roller-coaster, not realising how to stimulate the desired mental state – a state of such resourcefulness that it leads to sustained success.

It is the associations in your mind that are the key here. The images we carry around in our subconscious mind reflect like a wave in our lives, like ripples in water they impact on everything we say, do, are. They have a huge impact on the way we act, even at a subliminal level, almost imperceptibly.

So, in order to reach for better results and new levels of success, via improved performance, and behaviour, we must first upgrade the images we are carrying around in our mindset: to reprogramme the subconscious.

Now, I haven't suddenly turned into some scary mind twister who is going to brainwash you. Remember, the thought-print is already a result of programming. All we are doing is influencing the programming to create the actions required to reach the results desired. To do this, we can use some specific psychological performance techniques: the sort of thing top sports stars use to enhance their belief and heighten performance. I call these Visual-is-ACTION techniques.

VISUALISATIONS = Visual-is-ACTIONS

Now, the techniques throughout the book are all tried, tested and proven tools that are immediately useable, highly practical, and definitely effective: I know, I have seen them in action.

They are not a 'quick fix', but you will see some very tangible and specific changes within the first 28 days of using them.

Here are the fundamental principles for all of the Visual-is-ACTION techniques:

1 The mind cannot tell the difference between what is real and what is imagined.

2 Seeing is believing. And we can only achieve what we believe. Therefore, if we see it, we can believe it and achieve it.

3 The images we carry around in our heads have a huge impact on the way we behave, on our performance and, therefore, on our results. If we carry pictures around in our mind of success, we will start to behave in a way that is consistent with that success and we will get results that are consistent with that success.

4 The subconscious is very child-like: very literal. What we feed in is believed. We need to feed in the right imagery and associations to give it the correct commands that are commensurate with the results we are aiming for.

5 What we feed into our subconscious controls our behaviours at a habitual level – and we know that successful people are those who have successful habits.

6 If we don't feed the subconscious in this way, it will seek other associations and make up an ad-hoc set of beliefs that will determine our behaviour.

Now, some people think they can't visualise because they don't imagine things in full cinemascope or like a 3D film. Perhaps they think in a different way, based on gut-feelings, on sounds, or, more likely, a combination of senses. Let's be clear: when I use the term 'visualise', I don't just mean the pictures. It's also about the feeling you generate. So 'visualising' a future goal is not just about creating pictures of it. It's about creating a greater sense than that.

Visualisation → VisualisaCtion → Visual-is-ACTION

That's why there's one other element to these Visual-is-ACTION techniques. Creating pictures is one thing, but getting inside those images and playing them out as real episodes in your mind's eye is the key. You see, it's how you 'C' them. Without the aCtion element, they are just fanciful day-dreaming. Add action, and they become a vignette playing out in your mind, a scene that the mind believes to be real. The mind is engaged with it happening, and the level of belief increases.

Of course, it's not simply a question of sitting around playing mind-tricks, and idly day-dreaming and using secret wishing techniques. The mind has to genuinely believe in it and, for that to happen, it requires as much of the surrounding conscious evidence to support the new mindset as possible. Whilst the subconscious can hold onto the belief from the Visual-is-ACTION technique, we can provide additional external, tangible evidence to help it believe even more.

We'll cover the specific Visual-is-ACTION techniques I use throughout the text. As you will see, these are all very simple techniques that will upgrade your mindset, ensuring enhanced performance, better results and more success – sustained.

Chapter key points

What you believe you can achieve. What you see you believe. It's easier to achieve what you see.

■ High achievers have the habit of 'counting their chickens'. They expect to succeed.

■ Most people have limiting beliefs, which affect their day-to-day behaviours, affect their habits, affect their actions and, in turn, affect their results.

■ In order to create success, we need to start by working on mindset – creating strong mental images of your future success allows you to programme your subconscious to believe you will achieve it.

Action Zone
Time to download

My 'Achiever's Mindset' Action Zone

What I have learned	What I am going to do about it

CHAPTER 3

Taking Personal Responsibility

'Nothing so conclusively proves a man's ability to lead others as what he does from day to day to lead himself.' THOMAS J WATSON

Creating results starts with what I believe to be the most fundamental, common denominator that all successful people believe, and practise:

TPR: TAKING PERSONAL RESPONSIBILITY

The mindset of the truly successful achiever in any walk of life is:

'If it's to be, it's up to me.'

No one else is going to do it for you. You have to take personal ownership of a project, goal, result. No one is going to build your business for you, stop smoking for you, get fit for you, make your sales for you, lead your team for you.

Success is not a destination, it is a journey. Taking personal responsibility for that journey, *your* journey, is the first step. Many people never take that first step. They are left hanging around at the start line wondering when/if it's all going to change for them.

If we have no goals, no purpose, there is a vacuum left in our subconscious. And because nature abhors a vacuum, all the attitudinal raw sewage, bad news, negative influences and problems pour in. Faced with this distortion, there's a tendency to seek external factors, and often other people, to blame. This leads to a life filled with blaming, complaining, grumbling, whinging and whining, where nothing is right, nothing goes right, and failure becomes a self-fulfilling prophecy.

Many people have a failure mentality which revolves around a story they tell themselves along the lines of, 'Well, I would be able to do x if I wasn't held back by y.' They find outside influences, or personal circumstances and see them as reasons why they are not able to do x. Let me tell you this: there is no one who has ever had the perfect straight run to the success line. Success is simply finding the way to overcome the challenges. There would be no achievement without the challenges. Everyone faces challenges. It's how you face them, how you see them, and how you respond to them that counts.

Responsibility = Response-ability

Literally, 'the ability to respond'. Note: *respond*, not *react*.

Most people, on a day-to-day basis, are reactive – they are rarely proactive in making things happen, decisively choosing a route, planning their day, their life.

And in micro-moments they *react* to events, to situations, to a set of conditions. Often these reactions are knee-jerk and negative. And often they revolve around 'blaming and complaining'.

To become responsible/response-able, let's move from reacting, to creating a response.

REA**C**TION ⟶ **C**REATION of response

It's all about how you 'C' it.

In every situation there are a number of angles from which to make your response. Some of these angles will provide helpful, proactive opportunities. Others will be a reaction, often knee-jerk, unhelpful and non-productive. The angle you take depends on how you see a situation.

The key is to know when you are creating a response. Successful people see every set of circumstances, every situation or event as an opportunity because they choose to respond, not just react.

When faced with a set of circumstances ask:

'How can I find a **P**ositive **R**eal **O**pportunity here?'

Let's call this Positive Real Opportunity Creation – PROCreation.

When faced with a specific situation or individual event, even a set-back, ask:

'How can I **C**reate a **P**ositive **R**eal **O**utcome to this?' Again, PROCreation.

Over-reacting and over-responding

The same goes for 'over-reacting'. Over-*reacting* is normally destructive. But over-*responding* is very different, and there are times when it's essential to over-respond in order to make a breakthrough, uncover an opportunity, and make a change.

For example, many successful businesses are started as a result of taking bold action in response to a specific situation. These are the people who, instead of grumbling when something frustrated them, spotted an opportunity, created a bold solution to the problem and established a compelling business – Richard Branson is a great example of someone who has done this repeatedly and, in most cases, found great success.

This approach is also the case in respect to learning life's lessons.

Think of the many times in life where you have had to keep relearning a similar lesson. Those times when you keep just falling short of what you want to achieve. Often it's the same lesson being repeated. And, if you identify the lesson that keeps on repeating itself and holding you back, you can fix it.

Maybe it's a lack of personal organisation, a failure to delegate sufficiently, a failure to keep up with your exercise regime, a failure to maintain loving relationships, finish important tasks, or keep hold of money you earn. Maybe it all revolves around fear, holding grudges or jealousies, being too proud or over-promising because of a desire to be liked, trying to do too much at once, or not investing your resources wisely.

Life is a series of lessons and, in order to move forward from your current lesson, you must learn it. You will then be faced with a fresh lesson (no one has ever completed the whole course!).

The more the lesson needs learning, the bolder your response needs to be. Bold and, often, simple. It may take courage, but that's part of the lesson: truly learning the lessons, rather than simply attending the classes. By genuinely learning the lesson, by creating a bold response, you don't have to keep learning the same lessons time and again and tolerating incremental quagmires and frustrations.

A bold response, a PROCreative response, means the lesson is learned, and that will expose new, fresh opportunities.

There are a number of signs to watch out for to indicate that a lesson needs to be learned, ranging from the simplest episode to the most destructive levels of frustration. For example, if you are always late for important meetings, or if you are ill-prepared for 'emergencies', if you always have more month than money, if you always miss deadlines, if you always end up working late into the night to complete key projects, if you always intend to go on that run, get fit, lose weight, but never get round to it…

If these cause frustration, and mean you don't get the results you are capable of, it's time for a lesson and a bold response. These frustrations, if they keep recurring, are simply life providing a lesson you need to learn. Look out for the lessons, and engage with them, learn to notice what's frustrating you, and take bold steps to rectify the causes.

SPHERES OF INFLUENCE

One of the most significant barriers to the achievement of results is the constant deflection of focus. People become deluded by, or dragged into, things that they feel need attention.

Indeed, we have all seen people arrive at the office wound up by something on the radio (probably listened to whilst in a traffic queue, which adds to the 'winding-up' factor). This is not very conducive to focus and a powerful mindset to start the day. Those who are successful have a habit of distinguishing where their control and input is required.

There are certain things outside your sphere of influence, and it's important to decide what's inside and what's outside, and to ensure you don't allow your resources of time and energy to deflect outside what you can influence.

The Serenity Prayer
God grant me the serenity
to accept the things I cannot change;
the courage to change the things I can;
and the wisdom to know the difference. REINHOLD NIEBUHR

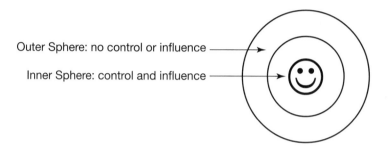

Outer Sphere: no control or influence

Inner Sphere: control and influence

Spheres of Influence

When faced with an issue, problem or challenge, decide whether it is in your sphere of influence and what you have influence over and can control. Then act on that. If something is outside your sphere of influence, outside your zone of control, don't waste energy thinking about it, talking about it, complaining about it, blaming it, or trying to act on it.

There are some things that seem to be outside your influence but, actually, on closer inspection, there are some aspects of them that you could bring within your sphere of influence. It's up to you to decide whether you want to act on these.

For example, you may not think you can control world poverty, human rights violations, or peace, or find a cure for cancer. These are outside your influence. But, you can bring such items within your sphere of influence, if you wish, and take action on what you can control, such as contributing to charities that tackle such issues. And perhaps deciding to contribute not just financially but by becoming actively involved. That then is a choice over how you act. It's not sitting around blaming and complaining. It's a proactive approach to issues that otherwise would be beyond your control.

As for those smaller aspects that are within your sphere of influence, well it's all about taking personal responsibility (TPR), and taking action.

When people take responsibility, take control and take action, it's great to observe the ripple effect in their lives – the positive waves that reflect through other areas they thought they didn't have control over.

FORWARD THINKING

To get really great results you need to change your focus and your thinking. To move forward you have to think forward and, as we know, that pesky furball of failure can get in the way of this progress. But now you know how to use those past failures as propellers to move you forward, you can then focus on forward thinking – thinking about the present/future in a proactive way, rather than being held back by thoughts based on the past/present.

*Your foreground is far more important
than your background*

Think about the fact that the whole of your future success, the whole of your future life, and everything you make of your life in whatever role from now on is down to you. You have absolute opportunity, absolute responsibility, absolute freedom. You have complete control of your thinking and, in thinking in the right way, you are creating a life consistent with what you want it to be. There's a Visual-is-ACTION exercise at the end of this chapter to help with this.

When you combine forward thinking and taking personal responsibility you will find that your mind creates pictures of the anticipated result in advance (especially if you also combine it with the Visual-is-ACTION techniques). I call this ability to see a finished result, and assess its impact, before it happens 'fast forward'.

Prevalent in all high achievers, this insight is extremely powerful for specific goals – the ability to spring the mind forward to the point where the goal has been achieved is like an instant mindset shift and, following on from the Achiever's Mindset (see Chapter 2), I'm sure you appreciate the power this provides.

EVERYTHING HAPPENS FOR A REASON

This is what all the successful people I've ever met believe.

They have a set view of coincidences and luck. Both are opportunities to be exploited, in the true sense. Opportunity is *everywhere* if you view the world through the filter of taking personal responsibility. And even when adversity strikes and 'bad stuff' happens, it obviously happens for a reason. It is part of the great story being lived out.

Opportunity is NOWHERE
or
Opportunity is NOW HERE

?

Opportunity

There are numerous examples of people who are in dire straits, whose lives are full of relentless challenge, but who view these minor, temporary setbacks as being merely a lesson to prepare them for the next stage of the journey, a necessary experience to allow them to grow and move onto the next stage, or a test – an opportunity to excel and be brilliant. Adversity is simply part of the journey. The adversity is the success.

SOME EXERCISES TO HELP AT THIS STAGE

EXERCISE

Visual-is-ACTION: THE FORWARD THINKING ARROW METHOD

On an index card (6 x 4 inches approx.) write the following:

Forward thinking

versus
Backward shrinking
Whinging and whining
Blaming and complaining

Hold the card about 9 inches away.

Focus on the point of the arrow. Look at the very tip of the point.

Don't read the card, but be aware of the fact that forward thinking will lead you to a fulfilled, exciting future.

Imagine you are at the tip of that arrow, ready to move forward and on to new heights of achievement. You are not held back by looking back. Imagine all the old clutter, the blaming and complaining, all the grudges you have held and feel have been held against you, all the 'fights' you have had, all the sourness and bitterness, all the 'unfinished business', getting smaller and smaller, fading into a small grey cloud, far away behind you, now miles behind you, and now like a minute black speck of dust, now diminishing and disappearing from view... completely.

You have left behind all the clutter, all the negativity, all the grudges and the jealousy. You are free of all that. It is far behind you. The new you has taken over... and it feels fantastic to be looking forward, to be moving forward. And, yes, you are now moving forward... imagine you are travelling on that arrow, gliding forward in a very exciting adventure, that is your life. And feel confident in what it holds for you. Imagine the arrow is propelling you effortlessly forward.

You only see forward... unleashed to move forward into new fields of golden opportunity... your journey is in your hands; you are responsible, and you feel responsible for your success... what a great feeling. And it feels so easy.

You now see stretched out in front of you the acres of opportunity, like golden wheat-fields stretching as far as you can see... left, right and to the far horizon, like warm, sunlit fields of fortune; vast tracts of possibility... and you can lead any way you like. It is immense, vast, warm and welcoming. And you can glide over it completely effortlessly.

COMMIT TO TPR

Write out an index card as follows:

> I am fully responsible
> for everything I am,
> everything I have,
> and everything I become.
>
> Signed ....

Sign the card and keep it safe. Read it every day.

Chapter key points

- Success is all about ordinary people doing extra-ordinary things. Step one is taking personal responsibility (TPR) for your success, and for the results you need to achieve on the way.

- You may be responsible *to* others, but you are not responsible *for* others. Don't let others put you off, don't be distracted or deflected from your own path. Each day is a gift for you and for your journey.

- TPR is the recognition that it is down to you to achieve all the results. It is for you to take action. All the blaming and complaining and all those things beyond your control use up your focus, energy, mental power. They detract from your results. There is no room for that 'stuff'. Time to get rid of it and get focused on what matters.

Action Zone
Time to download

My 'Taking Personal Responsibility' Action Zone

What I have learned	What I am going to do about it

CHAPTER 4

Playing To Your Strengths

'Whatever you are by nature, keep to it: never desert your line of talent.
Be what nature intended for you, and you will succeed.'
SYDNEY SMITH, 18TH CENTURY WRITER AND TEACHER

Lionel Messi, arguably the finest football player around today, does not go in goal. He sticks to what he's great at, mainly operating at the other end of the pitch and scoring goals. He leaves the goalkeeping to someone else who is best suited to it. In fact, if the Barcelona manager decided to play him in goal for a game, you can imagine how the crowd would react when they saw the team-sheet before the game.

Knowing your strengths, and applying them on a day-to-day basis, is critical for achieving results. Take a moment today to look back over the week, and ask, 'Am I playing to my Strengths?' Look at the amount of time you focused on your strengths and how much time was deflected into doing tasks that are not your forte, or into low-grade activity that doesn't correlate directly with your results and goals. Don't let yourself off the hook here. Be honest.

S/W SWAP?

When I ask people what their strengths are, they say things like, 'I'm *quite* good at this, and I'm *OK* at that.'

When I ask what their weaknesses are, they say, 'I'm *really* bad at a, b, c; and I'm *terrible* for being x, y, z.'

Interesting. We play down our strengths and emphasise weaknesses. Then I do a test, which I'll do with you now.

EXERCISE

Think of your strengths: write them down. Don't be shy.

Now, think of areas of weakness, the things you are not so good at. Write them down. Be honest.

Now, here's the test.

If I did a deal with you whereby I could give you a magic pill that would eradicate your weaknesses, *but* the side effect of the pill is that you lose your strengths, would you take the pill?

Of course not. Or at least I hope not.

The key to your success is recognising your strengths and playing to them, and recognising your weaknesses and finding ways to make sure they don't hinder you from your goals. You know, I've never had anyone agree to the deal.

Yet, most people spend their time worrying about their weaknesses, and that stops them exploiting their strengths. They fail to focus on their areas of excellence because they are too busy trying to improve their weaknesses.

BEWARE: CAPABILITY PARALYSIS

As well as undervaluing them, there's another reason people don't play to their strengths – capability paralysis. They mistake things that they *can* do for 'strengths'.

Due to technological advances and an increase in skill levels, we are now all capable of performing more tasks than ever before. But there is a downside. Too many people end up doing the 'busy' tasks. You know the ones that usually appear to be urgent, are easy to do and 'quicker to do myself', and crucially they rarely add any value to your work or move you forward towards a goal. They are also a distraction, lead to work overload, a lack of focus, procrastination and, ultimately, lower performance.

Now, look at the top people in your field. I'm pretty sure you'll find that they are not very good at these 'busy' tasks; you win there. However, they are very, very good at the important things that get them to where they want to be. That's because they have focused their energy and time on those actions and tasks that produce a result.

ABILITIES, SKILLS AND UNIQUE TALENT

'We are all born as infant prodigies.' THOMAS MANN

Abilities are innate; we are born with them.

Skills are learned, developed.

Talents are... well, there's one more component...

In addition to skills and abilities, your unique talent incorporates passion, too. Let's represent this in a simple diagram.

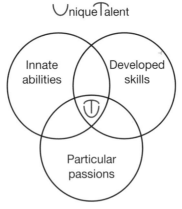

Successful people operate in the ∪ area only.
They play to their strengths, achieving results through *effortless power*,
rather than falling short with *powerless effort*!

Unique Talent Stratagram

The unique talent zone is where these three elements cross over; where there is a natural aptitude which allows you to take your innate abilities and develop a special skill, and have a particular passion for this area of expertise to the point of being one of the best in this field. This may be a combination of many abilities and many skills and, coupled with a passion, releases a desire to explode that talent.

> *'You've got to find what you love.*
> *Your work is going to fill a large part of your life, and the only way to be truly satisfied is to do what you believe is Great work.*
> *And the only way to do Great work, is to love what you do.*
> *Don't settle.'* STEVE JOBS

Consider the Unique Talent Stratagram – the intersection of your innate abilities, developed skills and particular passions.

Here are a few questions to help.

What is it that you:

- are very good at?
- find easy to do?
- see easily (i.e. you can immediately see that doing it would improve a situation)?
- are constantly told that you are good at? Think of those things you have done that people have said, 'You are really good at that sort of thing.' (Often they have asked for your help with something they can't do, and you can't help but get engrossed in helping them, and you find it effortless.)

- love doing?
- can't help graduating towards (i.e. it doesn't feel like work at all, in fact it's virtually effortless)?

'When love and skill work together, expect a masterpiece.'
JOHN RUSKIN

ACCESSING YOUR UNIQUE TALENT

It is estimated that, in any field, to develop the skills to achieve world-class expertise takes 10,000 hours of practice. So, to be at the top, you will need to invest time. When those skills relate to your unique talent, it means you will continue practising because it's a particular passion – you are more likely to do it if you love doing it, as anyone who has struggled to learn skills they didn't have a passion for will tell you.

In terms of accessing our abilities, everyone has a huge subconscious machine that can do extraordinary things. Research into the world of savant genius has consistently shown that we can do extraordinary maths, extraordinary art, feats of extraordinary memory, if we access that part of the brain. Yet, under normal circumstances, those functions are masked by the conscious activity of daily brain work. You see, when you catch a ball, you are not aware how the brain is performing the calculation that allows you to judge the trajectory and make the catch. Experiments have shown that, when we turn off the 'conscious noise', the unconscious part of the brain allows us to perform such complex, extraordinary feats at an extraordinarily high level.

This, of course, has many ramifications for our own search for peak performance, and extraordinary success in whatever field. It is about allowing your talent to function, because it is what you, deep down, want to do, can't help doing, and won't be distracted from doing. And finding that you can put in the best hours of skill development possible.

Mask the conscious and allow yourself to do what you know in your heart will lead to success – to go with your talent. The Visual-is-ACTION tools we use will allow your subconscious to expose your innate abilities, your inborn genius.

'People say I started with nothing. They are wrong; I started with all there is.' HENRY FORD

Around five years ago, I had an experience that taught me something I'll never forget about the fundamental starting point for discovering how to get your best results.

Every three months I used to head into a recording studio to record the latest CD for my clients and workshop members. Stuart (studio owner/manager/musician and excellent recording engineer) has bags of talent in this whole area. And, on this occasion, one particular moment caught my attention as something to recount.

We talked about having a background musical chord sequence with one of the 'live' exercises on the CD. Swivelling around in the chair at his console, he turned to an adjacent keyboard, and said, 'You mean something like this?' and promptly knocked out a perfect piece, recorded it, added some effects and laid it onto the recording in a heartbeat.

I complimented him. He became embarrassed and, although you could see he was rather proud of his creation, almost rebuffed my praise by saying, 'Oh well, it's easy, y'know, anyone can do that… nothing special…'

Isn't it incredible how we always underestimate our own talents and view them as worthless? We assume that 'anyone can do that', so natural does it seem to us. We take for granted that, because we are particularly good at something, then everyone else, similarly, must be good at it. So we often ignore the opportunities our talents provide.

In the case of small businesses, this can affect the pricing of goods and services dramatically. And, in large corporations, sometimes individual talents remain hidden for years, frequently never really emerging.

For many, individually, it means they live a life that is so far short of their true potential, and the world is a poorer place for it. Often, people don't have the confidence and courage to pursue their talent, to capitalise on it, to exploit it to full capacity.

The future belongs to those who can package their talents and turn them out into the world as a product or service from which others will derive value. We are constantly told that we live in a knowledge economy. Yet I believe this is more about know-how. The future belongs to those who embrace the know-how economy in the New World Order by turning their talent out into the world, without fear.

Most importantly, when we are doing what we are great at, we are more likely to get the required results, because we will put in that extra ounce of energy, focus, time. This is why exposing our unique talent is the next step on your journey to achieving greater results.

Chapter key points

- When playing to your strengths, and in particular your unique talent, you will create results more easily. You can't help creating results, in fact... it comes without thinking!

- You do know deep down that you have all the ability, all the strength, right now, to allow you to be successful. You really do. Whether you deploy those strengths and, in particular, follow that unique talent, is a matter of choice.

Action Zone
Time to download

My 'Playing To Your Strengths' Action Zone

What I have learned	What I am going to do about it

CHAPTER 5

Goal Setting → Goal Getting

'The more intensely we feel about an idea or a goal, the more assuredly the idea, buried deep in our subconscious, will direct us along the path to its fulfillment.'
EARL NIGHTINGALE, MOTIVATIONAL THINKER

It's difficult to feel you are getting anywhere, if you haven't got anywhere to get! Goals are the key to helping you move forward, to making the changes required. When have you/ has anyone ever failed when they put their whole heart, mind, soul, energy, time, desire, belief, commitment, ability, skill, talent into the achievement of something? That's right, never.

All human beings are goal achievers. Automatically. And we feel truly fulfilled as human beings when we are engaged with a personal goal – something that's truly important to us.

The best results are gained from powerful goals where we feel fully engaged: mind, body and soul. These are the goals that drive you with a sense of desire, belief, commitment and urgency and harness your unique talents and skills.

I'm sure you can think of a time when this happened for you. Whether it was an exciting work project, a family event, starting a business, going on a big health kick, organising an expedition or collaborating to help solve a problem.

Remembering that time, can you also remember how driven you were, almost to the point of obsession? These are the projects that happened through pure force of your will and, boy, I bet it felt good.

> *Now imagine if you could bring that energy, commitment, belief and desire to every goal because when you do that you can't fail*

The key is in finding the goals that unlock those energies in us; that activate the natural achievement mechanism, to trigger belief, overcome the success reluctance, the fear, and go for our vision. This is what creates our greatest results. This is the stuff that differentiates the average from the exceptional and, if you ask anyone who has achieved success how they did it, this way of goal setting would have been crucial.

'Man with no target, hit nothing.' OLD CHINESE PROVERB

F-O-C-U-S ON PURPOSE

There's one word that always comes up when people speak about getting results: FOCUS. As an acronym, it could stand for:

Follow

One

Cause

Until

Successful

We must have goals in order to focus, otherwise it's just concentrating, and that's a very different thing altogether. People can be concentrating, but not getting desired results, because it may be that they are concentrating on low-grade activity that doesn't lead to results, to goals, to purpose and success.

Goals create context for results. Without goals, and a sense of purpose, success will always elude. In particular, our goals must feel like a 'cause' – a reason for taking action that leads to specific results, not just a target. And, that cause must revolve around our values, as individuals, as teams, as businesses. This is about having a fixed purpose – as an individual that's your primary purpose – the one big goal that encapsulates your values and the reason behind your life. As a team or a business, it follows in the same way – a primary purpose is what binds the team/business together, its raison d'être, encompassing its values and mission. It's your 'cause'.

> **Cause and effect**
> *The only way you can be effective is to have a cause*
> *To be at your most effective, you must have a cause*

Most training courses and goal-setting books will talk about SMART goals and complex goal-setting methods, timelines and extensive project-management-style planning structures.

Yet, I've noticed that successful people don't do it that way at all. They don't follow the traditional approach. In fact, at first, this rather threw me off track. How can they be achieving when they aren't even following the formula/ doing it the 'right' way? Surely, they have found a short cut! That's why many successful people appear to be mavericks, almost breaking the rules and conventions on success.

What I observed, and you may recognise it too, is that they tend to focus on long-term vision, a cause, and then go hell-for-leather at action to achieve certain short-term goals. They have a clear overriding purpose, and then focus on making immediate breakthroughs, rather than laying everything out in a long, drawn-out project-management schedule. They do things that create immediate impact and have a lasting effect.

To focus on getting the goals, not just setting them, our goal setting must:

1 Be big

2 Be MaD

3 Avoid confusing the 'What' and the 'Why' with the 'How'

4 Be less training room/HR department-like, and more emotionally challenging

5 Have timeless visions

6 Be definite

7 Be imbalanced

8 Start from macro to micro

1 Be big

Three stonemasons were at work when a stranger wandered by. The first stonemason was toting rocks to a pile, near a wall. 'What are you doing?' said the stranger. 'Can't you see that I'm carrying rocks?' said the stonemason. The stranger asked the second labourer, 'What are you doing?' 'I'm building a wall,' he replied. A few steps away, the stranger came upon a third stonemason. 'What are you doing?' he asked. This worker smiled and said, 'I'm building a cathedral.'

> *Big goals excite the subconscious*
> *They create compulsion*

When set properly, goals are a *cause* to fight for, an ideology, packed with values and beliefs that generate motives for action – reasons to get the results we want. The trouble with the way many people set goals is that, rather than inciting exceptional performance, they actually impose limits on performance.

> '*The greatest danger for most people is not that they aim too high and miss, But that they aim too low, and hit.*'
> MICHELANGELO

Let's just understand some of the fundamentals of getting results through peak performance.

There are so many incredible stories of achievement and human brilliance – the power to overcome adversity, the ability to rise to a challenge and the sheer humanity of that unique skill of capturing an opportunity. You will be able to think of many for yourself, stories of amazing feats, in sport, business, indeed any field where the boundaries are pushed beyond what is considered the range of 'normal'.

In short, there's an infinite boundary to what you are capable of. The only limits are those that we impose ourselves. If someone has done it, or something like it, it shows it can be done. You have to believe now that *you* can do it and that you *will* do it. In the same way as when Roger Bannister ran the first 4-minute mile, a feat previously thought impossible – a real barrier to all athletes, and then, within a year, 32 other people achieved the same.

Success is about ordinary people doing extraordinary things. Raise your own imagination level and believe in your abilities. You really do have practically limitless potential.

> *'So many of our dreams at first seem impossible, then they seem improbable and, then, when we summon the will, they soon become inevitable. If we can conquer outer space, we should be able to conquer inner space too.'* CHRISTOPHER REEVE, SUPERMAN!

We need to expand what the mind is conceiving we are capable of. Here's an exercise to do just that.

Step 1
On this side of the boundary describe what you would see as such an impossible dream for you, your life, your career, your business. Put as much detail as possible – the idea is to think so big it feels impossible.

Step 2
Describe the vision one step back from the boundary – almost impossible (and therefore possible!) – a considerable stretch in imagination. Concentrate on the results of that vision – what it means to be there, living that life.

Infinite Boundary Stratagram

2 Be MaD

When people are aiming at a major goal, it can be accompanied by a chorus of 'You must be mad!' We hear people say it all the time when they see someone aiming for a bold breakthrough, and even when they actually achieve the goal. In fact, we often chuckle to ourselves when we know we are aiming high!

Perhaps that is the secret ingredient. For you to consider it a worthy enough *big* goal, you must sense that others would say, 'You must be mad!'

Certainly, doing what others would consider 'mad' always seems to produce fantastic results. In this context, doing what is 'mad' is taking a challenge head on, persisting, going the extra mile, which most people would never tackle, or couldn't imagine taking on.

It is no coincidence that MaD also stands for 'making a difference'. And getting results is all about making a difference. So here is a question:

What are you doing, right now, that is in the 'MaD' category?

3 Avoid confusing the 'What' and the 'Why' with the 'How'

The What and the Why: the goals.

The How: the strategy/plan.

Making goals big also makes them less bureaucratic/ managerial in style and more action-focused and leadership-centred. And, yes, *dynamic*.

Setting goals is not project planning – that comes later.

When setting the big goals don't let the 'How' limit the goals, especially the purpose and vision, or strangle any prospect of removing the current limits you are operating by.

Separate the purpose (the why and the what) from the plan (the how). The plan is simply a set of actions (each leading to mini goals and waypoints) on the journey. The big goals, such as your primary purpose, are key at this stage, in fact at every stage.

For most people, they start setting goals, but very quickly settle into the planning role (it's that need to compartmentalise, to make logical), the how, which strangles ambition and limits expectations of performance. And, for now, we need to heighten ambition, to expose and explode our true potential by finding goals that we can be obsessed by, that drive our emotions and senses, that make us deploy our total focus and dedication.

4 Be less training room/HR department-like, and more emotionally challenging

I'm now going to give a big kick to the basic tenet of goal-setting theory and tell you to abandon SMART goals.

For a start, two of the letters stand for **A**chievable and **R**ealistic and, as we've already discussed, I want you to think *big*, be MaD and go for the impossible, not dally with the normal and achievable: that way lies mediocrity.

As Mr George Bernard Shaw so wisely said: '... all progress depends on the unreasonable man'. So, be unreasonable, set big, challenging, clear and compelling goals and you will remove any limits on performance, and that's what we want, because that leads to the actions that lead to the desired results and then to the success we want.

Goals also need to be full of imagery, full of challenge, to create an emotional attachment and desire, to conjure up energy and enthusiasm, and urgency to get things done. They also need to stretch us to do better, otherwise we'll always stay the same. Goals are not just about measuring whether/when a target has been reached. Set in the right way, they are tools to enhance performance to help you achieve the results you want. This link between goals and their impact on performance is often overlooked.

So, recognise the personal dynamite that ignites you: a pilot light for the goals/vision/purpose. Create a reason, a reward that is highly personal.

This is all about a change of approach. These bigger goals create a different intensity of purpose and different action. It's about achieving a breakthrough versus just being slightly better.

5 Have timeless visions

'Long-term' goal setting is to be avoided because if we tell ourselves 'x' is a long-term goal, we simply push it away into the future and, in fact, that acts against us achieving it. It becomes too detached, too distant. For example, if your goal was to have £1 million by 2025, it wouldn't feel like something you need to get started on *now*.

That's why, at this stage, we are not looking at goals in that traditional sense, with timescales on. Calling goals 'long term' pushes them away. We want to bring them closer.

In fact, we want to set a time on them that generates urgency. So, by all means set the time at a date, and then imagine achieving the goal at that date, *as if you were achieving it now.*

Our goals need to hold attention. And they won't if they are set as 5-, 10-, 20-year 'projects'. Our natural tendency is to allow them to slip out of sight shrouded by all the urgency of day-to-day urgency.

So, we need a compelling subconscious focus on vision, and an immediate focus on short-term breakthroughs that are in the context of, and consistent with, that vision. We'll come back to this when we look at awesome special missions (ASMs) (see Chapter 8).

My toes curl when big institutions say things like, 'Our mission is to become the number one bank for customer service.'

Why? Let me explain.

Goals must have meaning for how you act *today*. Which is why I recommend putting your goals into the present tense.

You see, when big institutions say things like, 'Our mission is to become the number one bank for customer service,' my first thought is why 'become'? Surely better to say: 'Our mission is to *be*...' or 'Our mission is *being*...' in the compelling present tense. Stating goals in the present tense provides:

- A real sense of identity, particularly important for teams – we are doing it now, together.
- Commitment.

- Excellence in performance. It's about being the *best* you can be, now, not just 'trying' to be the best, some time in the future.

- Belief. It makes the dream feel possible, and you'll immediately *feel* more successful, because the mission feels relevant to today.

Any *cause* needs to be right here, right now, living and breathing every day.

Martin Luther King said: 'I have a dream *today*'. Note: not a goal, a *dream*. And not some time in the future, *Today*.

How much of today is a reflection of your vision? Is your present determined by your past, or driven by your vision? Vision is not something for the future. It's something to drive the now, in a compelling, excited way.

6 Be definite

In the way they are stated, goals must have a clear definition.

So, not 'trying' goals! The goal is not 'to *try* to do x', it's 'to *do* x'.

If the goal is to 'try' to do x, then, as soon as you have moved a muscle in the general direction of x, you have 'achieved' the goal. You have tried.

In fact, what you are saying is that the goal is not to achieve x, but to not achieve it, because 'trying' means that the focus (the subconscious association) is in the struggle of working towards it, not of achieving it.

Clarity and simplicity are also important here. By many, 'clarity' is often translated as 'you must write down your goals'. Yes. That's true, in some ways. But the objective is not to have written goals. The objective is to have clear goals. Now, at this stage, that might sound like mere semantics, but it will make a difference later on. Because writing goals does not in itself create clarity. Nor, on its own, does it create commitment.

However, to be compelling, goals must be clear and, for most people, that means 'visible', hence the term visions, more of which below.

7 Be imbalanced

Work–life balance is a phrase I'm dead set against. It presupposes that work and life are on opposite sides – diametrically opposed. And, yet, if you are playing to your strengths, operating in the unique talent zone, with purpose and goals, work/business is a facet of your life. It's very much part of your life.

Focus and balance cannot mix in this context. The word balance is often applied to goals by trainers or by those who say things like, 'Yes, but you've got to be balanced.' This is often a 'cop out' because, for real achievement, absolute focus and energy are needed. And that is *imbalanced* in favour of achieving a result! Think of top athletes or performers: they often appear obsessive in their pure focus on achieving their goal and this is the key factor in their success.

Remember, it's your balance – your focus – based on your values. If you set the goals in the right way, with your life's purpose and values at the core, you create the foundations that allow you to be unbalanced without falling over! The imbalance is a choice, for you to take.

8 Start from macro to micro

To turn goal setting into goal getting, start from macro goals and move to micro goals. This provides context, at all times.

If I said to you we were going to meet up next week and start planning to climb a mountain, the first question you would ask is, 'Which mountain?' The answer informs all decisions from that point: how much training, logistics, and so on. It's a very different proposition to be setting the goal of climbing Everest, from simply going for a stroll on a local foothill. We'll return to this analogy later.

The point is, that goal-getting is not just looking at micro goals for today, or even for the week, month, year, or focusing on what's just in front of you. The bigger context is always there, like subconscious wallpaper, a psychological screen-saver. In the background, but informing the foreground.

So now that I've debunked the received wisdom on goal setting, here are the new rules for goal getting.

THE GOALS HIERARCHY

Primary purpose – the reason you are here, includes your values.

Mission – a specific manifestation of purpose, written down in the present tense.

Vision – a specific image of a life living that purpose. This also includes a strategic objective, encompassing very specific, tangible elements.

Strategy/plan – a series of waypoints, each of which may be a goal. We'll talk about the strategic plan later (see Chapter 6 – The Master Plan).

Awesome special missions – short-term, breakthrough goals (see Chapter 8).

EXERCISE

QUICK-FIRE VISION BUILDING

1 Magic wand question – if I had a magic wand for your life, business, career, team, what would you wish for?

Write down or mindmap all the things that come to mind immediately.

2 Let's have a time travel talk. Imagine we are meeting five years on from now and we are catching up with all the marvellous 'magic wand' things that you have done, describe them aloud.

Play this game with someone, and don't hold back. Set the conversation as if it has already happened.

Note: think five years, and then draw it forward to three years. That way you get to allow your mind to think big, and then stretch your mind to believe it will be achieved more quickly, and that, in order to do that, you had better get started. That makes it compelling to action and to look for opportunities that will immediately help you get there.

3 Write a fast forward journal entry for five years' time.

'My life/business/career on... date'

4 The radio interview. Imagine it's three years on from now and life/business/career has been fantastic for you. So much so that you have been invited to give a radio interview explaining your achievements. Play out that interview; describe vividly all the great things you have achieved.

In all these cases, note colours, feelings, sense in gut as you describe the goals already achieved. You might end up with something that looks like the vision stratagram overleaf.

Now make it colour-coded, and certainly use engaging phrases and emotive words to describe the ideal vision.

'Our true voyage of discovery begins not in seeking new lands, but in having new eyes.' MARCEL PROUST

Vision Stratagram

If I had a magic wand...

Vision

Incorporating elements such as:

**Business regime   Clients   Service
Marketing engine   Structure   Location   Systems
Operations, products and services   Profile and reputation
Financials   Lifestyle   Team/people   Time/freedom**

EXERCISE

Visual-is-ACTION: THE LIFT TECHNIQUE

This technique follows the principle for all the Visual-is-ACTION techniques:

- The mind cannot tell the difference between what is real and what is imagined.
- If we see it, we can believe it and achieve it.

- The images we carry around in our heads have a huge impact on the way we behave, on our performance and, therefore, on our results.

- The subconscious is very childlike: very literal. What we feed in is believed.

- Our subconscious controls our behaviours at a habitual level.

Begin by sitting in a comfortable seat, relaxed, with your feet flat on the floor. Close your eyes. Take a deep breath... and gently let it out.

Now, imagine you are on the 20th floor of a plush hotel.

You get into the lift, or elevator.

Picture yourself standing there. You press the button for the ground floor and, after a moment, the lift begins to descend. You see the red light descending through the numbers... 20, 19, 18, and so on.

As the lift descends, you are relaxing gradually, all the way down from the top of your head to the tips of your toes. All the way down... to the ground floor.

When you reach the ground floor, picture the lift doors opening.

Imagine you turn right, through a set of double doors, into a room. And there you see the ultimate moment of your success, the epitome of success for you, a very specific scene or event happening that indicates your success... and you are surrounded by this event, and you are in it... it's happening, all around you... see the picture, feel it really happening.

Play this scenario in your mind for around four minutes.

Return to the lift and get back in. Press the button for the 20th floor and the lift begins to ascend. You return to the 20th floor. Open your eyes and you are wide awake.

There's no doubt that this is a highly powerful technique. I have known people use this for just a few weeks and find that a goal they thought was at least three years off was achieved in three months... out of nowhere.

Remember, in order to achieve success, we first have to conceive that success in our mind's eye. Making our goals compelling is key to achieving results that lead to that greater success. The lift technique does simply that.

EXERCISE

TESTING YOUR GOAL-GETTING COMMITMENT

How committed are you to your goals? Here's one way of making sure the reasons for going for a certain goal are strong enough. I call this the 4X Stratagram.

It revolves around four questions:

1 What will happen if I do achieve this goal?

2 What won't happen if I do achieve this goal?

3 What will happen if I don't achieve this goal?

4 What won't happen if I don't achieve this goal?

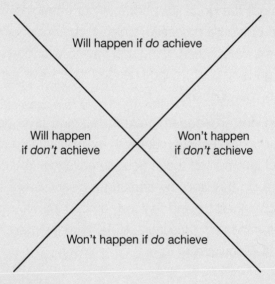

Will happen if *do* achieve

Will happen
if *don't* achieve

Won't happen
if *don't* achieve

Won't happen if *do* achieve

4X Stratagram

Fill in as many bullet points into the relevant quarter of the X.

You will know if the reasons are then strong enough to commit to the goal.

Commitment and desire to take action and get results come from the goals we have. They provide motiv-ACTION (motive = reason… for action) and, if set in the right way, provide a means of exceeding previous performance. If we focus them correctly, they enhance performance by tapping into those subconscious abilities and that resourcefulness we spoke of earlier.

Chapter key points

■ Goal getting is about deciding on, and committing to, the results you want to achieve.

■ If you set the goals in a compelling, engaging way, you switch on your true desire. Unleashing your energy, commitment, whole heart, mind and soul to your goals creates the high-level performance needed to achieve results that lead to your success.

■ This is not an academic exercise. High-level achievers have a certain engagement with their goals, and can 'see' the achievement of these goals in advance. You can learn how to do this, too, by creating a clear 'vision' that you are committed to, and that you embed into your subconscious mind using Visual-is-ACTION techniques, such as The Lift Technique.

Action Zone
Time to download

My 'Goal Setting → Goal Getting' Action Zone

What I have learned	What I am going to do about it

PART II

Get Set
Ready to move in the right direction

Having identified your goals, getting your approach right is crucial. Thinking decisively, identifying opportunities and setting up the first steps mean you will act in the right direction.

CHAPTER 6

The Master Plan

'Create a definite plan for carrying out your desire and begin at once, whether you are ready or not, to put this plan into action.' NAPOLEON HILL

So, you know where you want to get to, you have your goals, and you are raring to get going! Where to first? Well, you need a plan.

The Prussian strategist Clausewitz famously wrote: 'No plan survives first contact with the enemy'.

But we also know:

> *if you fail to plan, you are planning to fail*

It's really important to get the balance right between having a solid plan of where we want to get to (and how we are going to get there) and making it flexible enough.

A great plan guides you and ensures you stay on track. Being able to see where you are going generates confidence, particularly when things get tough, and gives us confidence to help make decisions, big and small, day to day because we know in which direction we want to head.

Now, for many, this is where the trouble starts.

Many people, teams, organisations and businesses over-plan: planning is such a cosy and comfortable activity that it becomes a displacement for taking action, a means of procrastinating, day-dreaming, wallowing in the vision. The planning can get in the way of creating the results you want.

Some are in a constant state of replanning. Some have so many plans for so many different ideas they forget which one is the real plan.

Just sitting around and hoping the vision will happen isn't enough, I'm afraid, and, similarly, running around taking lots of action is also not going to get you there. The action needs to be directed, built upon in a set route. So you need a master plan – an outline of how to get to your purpose/vision.

Those who get the greatest results have a knack of always keeping an eye on the goals, whilst taking massive day-by-day action. And they do this because they are always aware of the master plan. As any general knows, there's a huge difference between fighting battles and winning the war. The key here is to have a master plan of campaign, and not get diverted into meaningless, and unwinnable, battles.

Your master plan is borne of a few key principles:

V-P-A-R

Vision-Plan-Action-Result

The key is to move from vision to action. The P is simply the conduit to turn the vision into action that leads to desired results – vision into reality.

Planning is merely the vehicle that ensures our actions are building towards a set direction. Set the vision, have an outline master plan, and then take massive action, making everyone in the team accountable for action and results.

If you ever watch a professional snooker player, you'll see how potting the ball is one thing, but making the cue ball end up in position to pot the next ball, and the next, and the next is what marks out the best players. They can see several steps ahead – the very best can see the whole break laid out in front of them before they strike the ball. And, yes, if the ball doesn't end up exactly in position, they adjust the plan, and have to take steps to get on track, or they change the plan, but they do have a plan, that's for sure. And, just like snooker, each action on our plan has a result in itself, but also leads onto the next.

See the master plan as a journey, a route map.

A STRATEGY, NOT A STRAITJACKET

People talk of grand strategies, especially in business and, yet, sometimes a basic principle is all that's required. This informs your decision making enough for you to take actions and get results.

For example (and I've used this with many small-business owners):

Harley Street ←————————→ Wall Street

Are you aiming to be a Harley-Street-style business, or a Wall-Street-style business? A Harley Street business is one based on the expertise of specific individuals, all geared to one-to-one interaction with clients; and Wall Street business is big, transacting products and services with millions of customers.

It's a simplistic model, but I'm sure you get the point. Knowing which end of that spectrum you are aiming at is your strategy and that informs your master plan and your decision making every day.

Your master plan is a *strategy... not a straitjacket.*

Follow

One

Cause

Until

Successful

Note: follow one *cause* until successful.

Not: follow one *course* until successful.

The *course* may change, it may need to, because, in our changing world, adaptability is key. But the *cause* stays the same! Purpose/values/vision are constant. The route to getting there needs to be adaptable, flexible.

I hear lots of people say, 'I am at a real crossroads,' and they go on to explain the crossroads they are at and ask me which way to take. That is like taking someone out into the middle of the country, putting them at a road junction by a signpost and asking them which way to take, without indicating what the overall destination is. My answer is always to decide on your goals – they are the key to the plan.

OPPORTUNITY FOCUSED

We also want our plan to be flexible enough for us to slot in fresh opportunities as they arise. We would be foolish to ignore a genuine opportunity that takes us up our mountain just because it didn't fit in with the plan, or wasn't foretold. That's why the master plan is an outline, and simple, adaptable, flexible.

KISS – KEEP IT SIMPLY SIGNIFICANT

… and **K**eep **I**t **S**ignificantly **S**imple.

Significant: the plan incorporates a series of *bold* moves, on a specific track. The fact that you are working towards a set result, a set purpose, adds significance to your actions.

Simple: many people look for the 'complex secrets' to reaching new heights, rather than accepting the simple route, and getting on with it. I mean, we can be as creative as you like in gathering material for writing a book. There comes a point, however, when the writing must be done. Simple things are often ignored by people, who get wound up by complexity. In fact, simplicity is often discounted as unimportant.

The sad thing is that, when broken down into small steps, many people get bored of the actual actions needed to carry out their plan. So they stop.

Even though these actions in themselves are not very difficult, in fact they are probably rather simple, people just don't accept that it can be that simple. Many even look for something more sophisticated and complex to reach the goal, or some sort of trick or quick fix, rather than sticking to the simple master plan.

Success is simple, not easy, but simple. Don't allow yourself to be baffled by complexity. It's often the simple, big steps that are the most important.

MAKE IT A STUNNING PLAN

Many of you will be familiar with the film *The Shawshank Redemption*. Like all great films, it is riddled with messages, the most obvious of which is the value of sheer persistence and the power of hope in a vision. It also illustrates the value of having a stunning plan. Not just any old plan. Not even just a good plan. But a *stunning plan*.

And a stunning plan focusing on just a few key elements; the simple daily actions that lead to the big goal, when the whole plan comes together. The plan doesn't need to be convoluted, or complex. It can be very simple. But stunning in that, when you see the plan carried out, it makes you go 'wow!' It's also about creating a plan so bold that no one else would perhaps even contemplate it. Remember, bold. Not complex. Simple.

On a day-to-day basis, just as in *The Shawshank Redemption*, working your plan creates extra belief in your goal. No matter how small each step is, as long as it's towards the goal, belief can build.

Once you have your vision clear, your goals clear, and a stunning plan to take you there, work that plan.

THE WAINWRIGHT FACTOR

Occasionally a TV programme grips me. And one such occurrence was last year when I discovered a documentary about Alfred Wainwright, famed for his guidebooks to walking the Fells of the Lake District.

What was it that struck me?

Well, at first it was the complete obsession this chap had with walking the Lakeland Fells, and with documenting these walks through his sketches, maps and writings.

But the most astounding element was the way he went about it.

He set out a 13-year plan to cover all 214 walks. Yep. Thirteen years. Now that's a long-term commitment to any goal!

Having set out the plan, his focus, his energy, his resilience in carrying it out never came into question. So simple was the action required: walk every weekend, and write up the journals of the walk during the evenings each week (he was doing this part-time, whilst working as a town-hall clerk during the day).

Simple action. Not easy, but simple.

His obsession meant that this seemingly vast task was brought down to its most simple component actions. Actions that he could then focus on, day by day, knowing that in doing so week by week, month by month, year by year he was building to the achievement of his goal. In fact his passion for the mission was such that he didn't feel as if he had to focus on it at all. It felt completely natural to be doing it.

I bet there were tough times. I bet there were occasions when walking in the Lake District was not very comfortable, when the weather was not conducive, when he was not feeling so well, or when there were a thousand reasons not to do it.

But that wouldn't faze him. His goal was clear. And his plan was clear.

And did he achieve it? Yes. In one week short of 13 years. First of all, that's quite a plan... so very accurate. And second, it's an incredible execution of the plan.

Sticking to the plan was made easier because it was so simple, and because he was focused on his unique talent. With his plan in place, all that was required was to carry it out...

The lesson: plan the work, and then work the plan.

THE MOUNTAIN

Always plan from general to specific – macro to micro – from purpose and vision to immediate goals and first steps. The key is to make a simple plan, with waypoints marked as strategic goalposts.

Remember the mountain analogy we used earlier in relation to goal getting (see Chapter 5). So, let's just renew that reference using the principles we've covered here, to create your master plan.

Begin at the top: with the vision, you've got to know which mountain you are climbing before you decide how you are going to climb it.

Then identify the 'base camp' – what needs to be in place to allow you to make the launch to the summit.

Then identify the first steps to get there.

Remember, we are planning from macro to micro again, just as when we set goals. In fact, the master plan is simply a series of goals, waypoints and actions; a set of results that will take you up the mountain.

Yes, there will be a lot of 'ifs'. Each stage is contingent on the last – the strategy is always full of ifs.

> ### The middle word in life is If

A master plan, a stunning strategy, is about satisfying the *ifs* that take you to the top.

Know where every action is intended to lead to, a result; and know how every action will be sustained: this is part of the plan.

If your plan includes actions that don't lead somewhere, or can't be sustained, think again. After all, we don't want to take steps up the mountain only to find we have slipped back again. Each step must be sustained, and a solid building block created up to the next stage.

As well as your overall master plan, leading to your biggest goals, this mountain method can be applied to any result you wish to achieve. Start with a clear vision of the end result, then set a 'base camp' – a strategic objective comprised of all the elements being put in place that allow you to launch at the summit, and then decide the first steps towards the result that need to be taken immediately.

The master plan should ensure that none of the spontaneity of goal getting is lost. Most people say they would like to be more organised, to feel more in control, and yet so few deliberately set a course and plan a journey through life. They end up on that hamster's wheel. The same can be said for any goal.

Mountain Stratagram

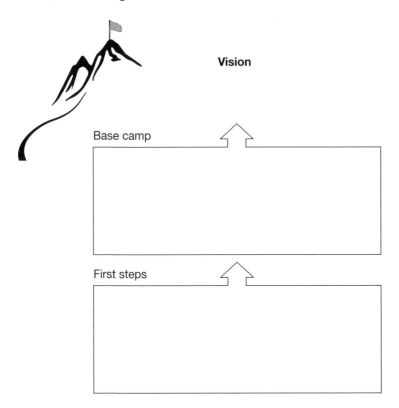

Vision

Base camp

First steps

The plan tells you where you are in relation to your vision. It allows you to get back on track by indicating what needs to be done next. It also frees you up to savour the moment, confident that you are on plan.

Chapter key points

- Once you know what your success is, your goals, you need a master plan – a strategic outline, an overview of the route to these goals.

- The best plans are simple, and retain flexibility to adapt to changing circumstances and to seize emerging opportunities. They are built on solid foundations, your values and your purpose, and point directly at your vision. But they are not a straitjacket.

- Keep your master plan simple and allow the actions you take and the results you get, every day, to have significance because they are following the course to your goals.

Action Zone

Time to download

My 'Master Plan' Action Zone

What I have learned	What I am going to do about it

CHAPTER 7

Generative Thinking

'I made an international reputation just by thinking twice each week.' GEORGE BERNARD SHAW

When you have a clear vision, a master plan, and a focus on the breakthroughs that will create the results you need to move forward on that plan, decision making on a day-to-day basis is much easier, and thinking of fresh ideas and opportunities also becomes easier. However, there will be times when you need to take stock, assess progress and consider fresh approaches, fresh options.

Someone recently came to me saying, 'All of our brainstorming and strategic meetings generate lots of discussion, but we seldom really create any concrete action. We don't get full value for the time taken out of the business by our highest-paid people.' A common enough complaint. It may sound strikingly familiar to you.

If you run your own small business, the challenge is the same. How can you find time to think strategically and put the new ideas generated into practice, whilst at the same time focusing on productivity; doing the day-to-day work that puts bread on the table?

We need to be thinking, creatively, coming up with fresh ideas to create results, so how can we think fast in order to translate that thinking into decisive action that gets results?

The secret rests with *generative thinking*; thinking to generate actions that lead to results. The four cornerstones are:

1 Time

It's no good sitting down once a year to 'think about ways of improving the business and the way we do things' to find that you stumble. Like any muscle, the generative thinking muscle will atrophy with lack of use. Exercised often, it will become strong. Setting aside time in your diary, on a regular basis, to think, without distraction, is one of the most important 'meetings' you can have.

If you don't set the time aside, something more 'urgent' will always crop up and you'll get to the end of a week, month, quarter, no further forward.

For those who run their own business, I have always advocated at least one full day per quarter as a 'hotel day' away from the business, purely for strategic thinking, as well as at least two sessions of one hour each invested in generative thinking every week.

2 Space

Find an environment that is away from your normal work space to get away from being in managerial or bureaucratic mode. So, not at your desk – a change of room, or even a separate comfy chair will help – away from any potential distractions – phones, laptops, emails, and so on.

Find a place where you can relax so you are more likely to access the brain waves that fuel creativity. These brain waves are most active when we are most relaxed. This is why so many people have great ideas when least expected.

3 Topic

Many people set aside the time and space to think, but then find themselves thinking about low-grade topics, or getting side-tracked into minor business issues. So, choosing your topics for generative thinking in advance is critical. Of course, your goals (or ASMs – see Chapter 8) and issues arising from their progress, will be prevalent topics.

Have some opening questions formed, such as:

- 'If we had a magic wand, and we waved it over the despatch department, how would we want that to run?' Or

- 'If we absolutely *had* to do x, how would we approach it?' Or

- It may be that you simply have a specific issue or opportunity that needs some decision time. So the topic could be: 'sorting out the website', or 'creating a strategic alliance with xyz ltd'.

Be challenging and opportunity- and solution-focused. The rules that apply to any meeting also apply here. The object of the exercise is not 'to discuss' or 'to think about', but 'to decide'. The thinking is simply the vehicle that allows you to take decisions and commit to action.

4 Tools

Too many people end up in meandering 'creative' thinking sessions. They soon realise they aren't getting anywhere, and stop thinking at all. It is important to make your thinking 'whole-brained', using both the logical, practical part of your mind as well as the emotional, creative part. It's not one *or* the other. It's both.

Have some thinking techniques that allow you to capture the ideas as they are generated. So, Tony Buzan's 'Mind Mapping', or Edward de Bono's 'Thinking Hats', or any number of tools will help. Most people think in pictures. And these don't have to be works of art, they can be very basic.

Nurture creativity. Being creative exercises the creative spirit. You can't sit down and say, 'Right, now I'm going to start being creative,' if you haven't exercised that muscle for years. Become creative by taking up creative hobbies or arts. That will strengthen that part of your mind so that you can apply it in business. Creativity is not something to be switched on and off. It's a mind muscle you develop, that you employ in tandem with all other aspects of your thinking.

Some specific tools

- **Mindsurfing**. Once a week, for about 45 minutes, this is a powerful session of generative thinking. It revolves around www.

  - **W**ow: how can we 'wow' our existing clients and customers? What improvements in service and products can we implement?

  - **W**oo: how can we 'woo' new clients/customers? What fresh marketing approaches can we employ?

  - **W**in: how can we 'win' as a team? What can be done to improve the way we perform as a team – our environment, our systems, our structure?

- **6-3-1 Brainstorm**. What are the six key areas of my business/career/life ?

  What three things can I do to improve each area?

  What is the one thing I am going to improve immediately?

- **Always think with a pen in your hand**. And use colour (those four-colour multipens are perfect for this).

  Just writing down the challenges you face, or the opportunities available will help you to find clarity. Using pictorial representations, or putting the options and solutions on a spectrum (with the extreme options at either end), will help you see how you can find the best solution and will make you more aware of the results you want to achieve, so the likely outcome of each action can be clearly seen.

- **Component parts**. Many people get overwhelmed by the size of individual tasks. This causes procrastination because the task seems so insurmountable that you simply can't think how to start.

  It is essential to break such major projects down into manageable chunks. Whether that's writing a book, a report or proposal, preparing a new product launch or breaking into new markets. Taking a bit of generative thinking time and breaking the project down only takes a short time, and breeds confidence in the project, as well as identifying the specific smaller actions needed. When you break it into chunks, keep in mind the result you wish to achieve.

  Once you have worked out what these chunks are, look for support, delegate, and then all you have to do is get on with it!

- **Inside the box**. A business owner was discussing with me the particular challenges he faces. He runs a professional service business, is technically very skilled, and he loves his clients. Great, so far.

  He wants to make a serious breakthrough, having plateaued somewhat in the past couple of years. His suggestion at first was that he needed to 'think outside the box' a little, to come up with creative ways in which to market his services and find new clients.

  However, during further discussions it became apparent that, whilst these are all wonderful approaches, the first thing he needed to do was to look much closer to home. In fact, he didn't need to 'think outside the box' at all. He needed to look *inside the box.*

When we looked at his practice, he was already sitting on lots of potential new business which just needed to be brought in. In a moment of complete honesty he agreed that the problem was that he just had not been doing the basics for some time. He had forgotten those activities that had been the foundation of building his business in the early days.

And I see so many business people doing the same. Thinking outside the box is all well and good, but sometimes it's worth looking at the 'inside the box' activities which will produce the results you want.

Look at all those sportspeople who succeed and you will see that their success is built on doing a few simple things consistently well, playing to their strengths.

I know loads of small businesses and sales people who know that their business will stand and fall on the ability to make contact calls to customers. That's *inside the box*. How many have perfected this and got seriously good at that one simple thing? Only the successful ones! And I sometimes wonder whether those who are looking outside the box are simply shirking doing the simple things.

- **The TV panel show**. Create a panel of people who you respect and admire. Choose between three and seven people to be on the panel: choose them for their different characteristics, whether it's Gandhi or Richard Branson.

  Have a chairperson to host the imaginary show. You might write their names down, or print off pictures of them to remind you. The subject is a particular issue, or decision, you need to work through. Allow the characters on the panel to discuss the issue and advise you. Notice who is saying what, and note it down. What do you agree with? What about your gut-feeling? Does it match your values and vision? Many fresh ideas and approaches can be elicited by this method and you may be surprised at which you favour.

- **Doing the opposite**. Remember, if you keep on doing what you've always done, you'll keep on getting what you've always got. So, what results are you getting that need to change? How about taking one thing that's not working, and doing the opposite as an experiment? The danger for many is that, by simply tinkering with what's not working, we never really change the results dramatically enough.

- **New legislation**. Let's play a little mind game. Imagine the government suddenly brought in legislation in your profession that everyone had to double their productivity within three months, or they would lose their licence to practise (hey, it could happen!).

What would you do? What sort of ideas would you have to come up with to stay in business? Posing these sorts of questions allows your subconscious to seek big, bold ideas and actions that it simply isn't looking for when the objective is a 2, 5 or even 10 per cent increase.

OPPORTUNITY OVERLOAD?

When the Vikings wanted to fully settle a new territory (rather than conducting a hit-and-run raid), they would burn their boats. Why? So there would be no going back. They were fully committing to conquering and settling for good. Having removed any thoughts of ever going back, they would have thoughts only of moving forward.

If you are one of those people who likes to have an escape route, something to fall back on, you may find it useful to learn a lesson from these Vikings. Are you holding onto that escape route so tightly you can't move forward? Are you keeping so many options open you can't take advantage of any of them?

This often happens out of fear, or lack of real commitment to the actions that need to be taken. It can lead to poor decision making, total indecisiveness and frequently the sufferer ends up doing nothing, neither fully committing to one route nor the other.

There must come a point when you decide on a definite course of action, as if it was the only course open to you. It's amazing the results we get and the success we enjoy when our only option is to take massive action in one direction.

> *More opportunities are lost through indecision than the wrong decision*

If faced with opportunity overload, take all your opportunities and run them through a simple vetting filter:

The ORGASM Stratagram

Opportunity: what is the opportunity specifically?

Reason: what is the reason this is an opportunity for you? How does it sit with your vision and master plan? Or is it an alluring distraction?

Goal: what specifically is the goal with this opportunity?

Affirmation: describe the goal as if it has happened. What will it look like, feel like, be like to have taken this opportunity and succeeded with it? Are you compelled by it?

Strategy: what series of actions needs to be taken to bring this opportunity to fruition?

Measurement: how are you going to measure each step?

If at any stage the opportunity loses its shine, take it off the list. It will become apparent which are the opportunities to pursue.

GENERATIVE THINKING 'ON THE HOOF'

In addition to the structured generative thinking sessions we've covered here you will soon find you are able to use the principles of generative thinking moment by moment, moving swiftly from thinking to action, because you have trained your mind to work that way.

You will find that, in every situation, you are looking for the objective, designing a route in your mind, being decisive and then taking action. It's like a mini mountain stratagram that you conjure up for generating results with everything you do: from important business phone calls to meetings, to writing proposals and reports, to practically everything.

With your vision, compelling goals and an outline master plan to which you are working, the thinking you do is much clearer, faster and more decisive; particularly if you are using the Visual-is-ACTION techniques covered so far, because your subconscious is also feeding you with ideas and gut-feeling intuition to help seek out the opportunities that lead to actions that generate the results you want.

The final step in generative thinking is to take immediate action. And I mean immediate. Right after the session, take point one of the resulting action plan and activate it. Do something immediately to get things on the move. That single action sends the signal that you have committed to the change.

Generative thinking is not about sitting back, allowing the thoughts to come to you and then hoping that one day you may get round to implementing 10 per cent of the ideas. It's about generating action, through thinking.

It also takes practice. Start now, you'll never regret it.

Chapter key points

- Think! Most people don't set aside the time and space to think properly. It's almost seen as 'day-dreaming'. Indeed, often it is, because people fail to generate decisions and actions with the thinking.

- Generative thinking is about setting aside the time, and creating the space, to devote to topics and ideas that require some analysis or problem solving.

- Deploy your thinking toolkit to decide on courses of action that lead to results, that keep you on course, along your master plan, and to identify and exploit opportunities that others are simply 'too busy' to entertain.

- Make thinking in this way a habit, and strengthen it like a muscle through constant use.

Action Zone
Time to download

My 'Generative Thinking' Action Zone

What I have learned	What I am going to do about it

CHAPTER 8

Awesome Special Missions (ASMs)

'Life is too short for non-"wow" projects.' TOM PETERS

BACK ON THE MOUNTAIN

Let's just remind ourselves of your overall master plan: your mountain strategy... get that piece of paper to hand right now.

Successful people build solid businesses and careers a piece at a time, aiming big and going deep on certain specific aspects. They are not trying to be everything to everyone, to do everything, to be a know-it-all, can-do-it-all. But they are always aiming to make whatever they are working on bigger, bolder, better, more. They aim at more frequent, greater volume, quicker. It's as if they only ever play one card, a card that trumps everything anyone else does. They never settle for average and they don't get distracted.

As we've already seen (in Chapter 7), opportunity overload leads many people astray, leaving them feeling overwhelmed by trying to take on too many new ideas. I have seen this happen to too many businesses that end up at a dead end. They are not decisive enough about the track to reach their vision, and end up trying to do too much, to do everything that comes along and appears to be 'worthwhile' or a good idea. Of course, having clear purpose and vision will help eradicate this. But there is another element, too.

We need to keep the pace up, to create breakthroughs to continue climbing our specific mountain. Successful people have a tendency to make *big*, *bold* moves – really decisive steps forward. And they take these steps on when others wouldn't. And they take them confidently because they know that they are helping them reach their big goal.

It's about focusing clearly on developing specific elements of your overall plan. So once you have that vision, the top of your mountain, and you have chosen base camp, the strategic objective, and all the components, once you have broken it down into clear specific elements which need to be in place, then build the big breakthroughs around these elements.

> *Involvement can be by accident. But commitment is always deliberate!*

Applying your resources and full commitment to these few significant breakthroughs will enable you to achieve far more than the person who looks for minor improvements and spreads themselves too thinly to make any real difference.

Well, now we come to climbing our success mountain. What are the bold steps we will take? Each of these is a goal in itself, and needs to be framed in a way that continues to inspire us: as an adventure to conquer the next challenge and as an opportunity to excel and have fun.

The human condition is to revel in these challenges, if presented in the right way. We want to have goals to achieve – we LOVE it – our spirit thrives on it. We are never happier than when we are working on something we really care about, that takes us into new territory of achievement. When given the opportunity to excel in this way, people rise to the challenge, often going way beyond what was previously considered possible.

Most people set themselves too many short-term goals, and they make the goals too small. They end up overwhelmed, without focus, and making only incremental progress. Successful teams, businesses, individuals, on the other hand, focus on making just a few big breakthroughs that have an immediate impact and a lasting effect. And that's how we are going to approach your first steps up the mountain.

LEAPFROG THE SUCCESS QUEUE... AND ACCELERATE TO SUCCESS

It is polite to wait one's turn in life. It is polite, and we do it pretty well automatically. And, in most circumstances, that's good. It is the right way to behave.

But when it comes to reaching your goals, to achieving success, a different approach is required. It is not about pushing others out of the way, of course. Far from it. Yet too many people stand around waiting for success to come to them. Many people cruise along doing what appears to be the right sort of things to 'make it to the top' but never making the bold breakthrough, the leap of faith. You see, people often get in the habit of cruising. Even if they are doing the right things, climbing the mountain, there's a danger that it will become a plod, when a great stride forward is required. And when you make that quantum leap forward, through a bold decision, a bold action, you leapfrog the queue of people in the 'mediocre zone'. So, it's important to zap up the intensity, to make bolder strides. Often, all that's required to reach the next stage on the mountain is a period of sharp action to lead to a specific foothold.

You may even be able to think right now of one specific short-term achievement that would catapult you up the mountain towards your vision right now. You know, if you want to build a business to the next level, how quickly could you create a whole new marketing platform? Or, if you wanted to engage a whole new market of clients, how quickly could that be done if real genuine focus and intensity was put into it?

Or, if you wanted to get fitter, or slimmer, is it time to approach this with absolute focus, rather than just a feint willingness? Bringing these specific short-term goals to the centre of your attention, to the centre of your life, is at the root of success.

It's time to pour your resources into this one area of action to power you up that mountain. It's time to stop cruising and accelerate to success.

What one thing could you do that will make you leap forward to your vision? Today.

ASMs

Having just a few big goals to focus on short term helps to *Keep It Simply Significant* (KISS, remember?).

At all times, if you know what your long-term vision is, when it comes to making real short-term breakthroughs, I suggest a 90-day focus on around one to three key 'projects'.

The term 'projects' is too dull a word for me, I'm afraid, and rekindles images of third-year geography lessons. Hardly dynamic! So, I use the acronym ASM, which stands for awesome special mission.

ASMs are short-term breakthroughs which unlock specific doors to lead to your long-term objectives.

Perhaps the best way to define an awesome special mission is that it must have:

1 an immediate impact (in terms of results – very specific and tangible);

and

2 a lasting effect. It relates to the prime purpose and strategic objective and has an impact on the overall long-term growth of, say, a business, a team, or an individual.

So why the term 'ASM'?

1 ASMs are 'Awesome' because they represent the accomplishment of stretching goals and significant feats. The target is big, and significant, and, to use the modern parlance, it is 'awesome'. Setting such a big goal should give you butterflies in your stomach. Some people think that is fear, and they shrink away from the goal and even dismantle it before they've started. But, that 'butterfly moment' is, in fact, the first sign you are excited by the goal. And that's critically important!

2 ASMs are 'Special' because we want to be proud of them – for the whole team to look back on them in years to come and say, 'Do you remember when we did x...', or for you personally to have a special pride in what you achieved.

3 ASMs are 'Missions' because they engage our hearts and minds. We care about them, deeply. We must be *compelled* to achieve them. They take absolute priority in terms of our focus, time, energy and investment. We must draw on *all* our resources to achieve them.

- Like military operations on a raging battlefield.
- Like the enemy machine-gun bunker which must be taken out, at all costs.
- Like the hostage siege which must be broken.

No place for faint hearts, or long, drawn-out meetings to think about, pontificate, postulate on what must be done next. Once the start line has been crossed it's all *action*. And all *productive* action. This is about overcoming major challenges, achieving speedy and effective breakthroughs. It requires bold action. And it requires you to super-perform at your elite best. In my experience, people do this best when a little pressure is on, when they are in a crisis, as long as they are compelled by the goal.

So, as an analogy, imagine you want to reduce your golf handicap from 24 to 22. You would probably book a few more lessons, and aim to play a little more often. OK. That's the norm. Now, imagine you want to reduce your golf handicap to single figures, or even to be a scratch golfer... zero handicap. Now, in the second case, your approach will be much, much, *much* different, won't it? Of course. A few lessons and a little extra practice won't cut it. It needs a revolution in approach. And that will need a revolution in performance. That butterfly moment, that gut-feeling of toppling over the edge into a zone of heightened commitment can be frightening, or exhilarating, depending on your viewpoint. But the results achieved will be totally different.

You see, there's an almost super-human focus and energy generated when people are passionate about a mission. They become absorbed by it, and nothing else matters. Because you are focusing on a few key breakthroughs, you can afford to think bigger, better and bolder. Focusing allows you to feel freedom and is in itself a motivating influence on your performance. You already feel better for getting clarity around what is important right now.

WHAT ARE YOUR ASMs?

What are your key goals right now?

In business terms, it could be:

- setting a particularly huge quarterly sales goal
- creating and launching a new website
- developing a new product and launching it to the world
- moving premises, taking on new people, overhauling the existing premises, offices, factory floor, business systems; or
- *completely* transforming the service you offer or breaking into a whole new market.

It may be that you can combine a number of smaller elements into an ASM. For example, one of my clients had a 'list of next things to do' which included 'getting website copy finished', 'signing off branding and logos', 'creating video for website', 'testimonials' and a number of other items. We turned this from a 'to do' list into a sense of making a significant step up the mountain by grouping all such actions into an ASM called 'platform creation' and set a challenging timescale. The approach became somewhat different and the levels of focus, intensity and compulsion to carry out each individual element in the set timescale took on more significance and meaning.

And your ASMs don't just have to be business-related.

For example, you might set a fitness ASM of, say, running a 10-kilometre charity run, or a marathon (depending on your starting level); even an ASM to clear your garden, or totally overhaul a part of your house, renovating and decorating specific rooms; even to learn a new language, write a novel – you know, the one you always wanted to get round to writing.

I recommend having a *maximum* of three ASMs at any one time. If you have three, one should be business or career-related, one personal and one other (could be either business, personal, or related to one of the other areas of your life).

So, what are your one to three most important goals *right now*?

Why not turn these into awesome special missions for the next three months? Here's how:

a Specify the vision – the outcome of the ASM in your mind's eye. What do you see, what do you feel as you achieve it? Make it compelling. Remember the child-like zest, absolute heart, mind, soul, body commitment to it. If it's not compelling enough, take it off the list.

b Is the ASM appropriate in that it is in line with your values and vision – aligned with your prime purpose?

c Is the ASM desirable? Do you really want it and are you prepared to commit everything to achieving it?

d When, where and with whom will you achieve this ASM?

e Specify the evidence. How will you know when you have achieved it? What will the evidence be? The hard facts.

f Is the ASM for you only, or does it involve others? If others are involved, let's get them committed by communicating the ASM in a compelling way, and collaborating with them. Get them on the team from the start.

g What resources are needed to achieve the ASM? And are you prepared to commit those resources? We'll talk more about resources later (see Chapter 12).

h What strengths, capabilities and know-how do you have already that will help you, and that you need to major on and bring to the fore to achieve this ASM?

i What blockers do you need to overcome? And how?

j Have you ever done something like this before and, if so, what know-how experience can you tap into? Or, if you haven't, do you know someone else who has? Can you access their know-how, learn from their experience and model what they did?

k Create an action plan: in outline what are the key steps to take to achieve this ASM? Can you identify specific actions that need to be taken, and specific timeslots for doing this?

l Can you create specific identity around this ASM? Give it a name? Does the team on this goal have a special name?

m Visualise the end result – already achieved. Write out the ASM, with powerful imagery focused around the completed goal. And commit to it by signing for it.

n And don't forget to set a reward for achieving the ASM.

Once you have set the ASMs, focus on them as priorities. Generate energy, enthusiasm and commitment to each one.

THREE LEVELS OF ASM-GETTING

One of the reasons people don't set goals, as we have said before, is that they think they are setting themselves up for failure.

When it comes to ASMs, this certainly comes into play. We want to be challenged and excited by our ASMs. We want them to create those butterflies in the stomach. That tells you it is an ASM (awesome, special and a mission) by definition. If it doesn't get those butterflies fluttering, it's hardly worthy of the title ASM. And don't let the excitement translate into fear.

Always remember, there are three levels of success in any goal:

1 *The achievement level*: this relates to the actual target, the result, the success of achieving the specific target.

2 *The performance development level*: the building of skills, character, ability, experience, developing of knowledge, the testing of performance.

3 *The learning level*: learning the lessons from the journey, from taking on the ASM, from the way you approached it, what worked, what didn't work, the development of experience and know-how, the growth of the individual and of the team.

And so, as you can clearly see, if you approach your ASMs as we have discussed, you will always succeed on levels 2 and 3, even if level 1 is not reached. You will be better equipped next time, anyway! In my experience, if the principles are applied, whole-heartedly, fully, the ASMs are always achieved.

ASMs are designed to set the butterflies off in your stomach. That's not fear, it's excitement. Don't shrink back from it. Embrace it. It is a sure sign that you are about to make a breakthrough!

And remember the MaD factor: You must be 'Making a Difference'!

And there's one more tool to help achieve your ASMs. In fact, it's a hugely important technique because it taps into that most powerful resource, our subconscious.

THE STAR CARD Visual-is-ACTION TECHNIQUE

As we have seen, the main key to enhanced performance is through subconscious imagery. The Visual-is-ACTION exercises all follow a very simple formula and, for ASM achievement, I have found that one specific technique works best. I call it the Star Card technique.

For this, you'll need a small piece of bright blue card (approximately 10 cm x 7 cm) and a gold star, like one of those stars children put in their exercise books at school. Stick the gold star about half a centimetre off the centre of the piece of card.

Here's how the technique works.

With your star card in your hand, sitting down, with your feet planted firmly on the floor, close your eyes, and relax from the top of your head, right down through your body, allowing that wave of freedom to flow down your shoulders, through your chest, your stomach, down your legs and out through your toes.

Open your eyes, remaining relaxed, and now take your star card and hold it approximately 20 cm away, in front of your eyes. And allow yourself to gaze into the star, as if you are defocusing on it, seeing through it.

And imagine what's in the star, what it represents, picture that moment of success when you achieve the one goal you are currently focused on – the ASM you are going for right now – that goal, that special mission you have set yourself to achieve.

Picture that goal, imagine that moment when you have achieved it, see as much detail as possible – the colours, the sounds, the touch of it. Imagine what is happening, as you achieve it. Play it out like a scene that has happened. Get that sense in your gut, of this achievement, your sense of reward.

Hold that thought.

Do this Visual-is-ACTION for around one minute.

And, as a small add-on to this technique, I suggest you get three or four of those gold stars and stick them in various places around your office or home. Just key peripheral areas, like on the corner of your laptop, or by your phone.

In addition, carry your star card around with you. Take very short glances (a couple of seconds) at it at various moments during the day.

What we have done here is used a very simple psychological trigger. You see, you already have a clear association in your mind between success, achieving a result and the gold star from an early age. This technique plays on that subconscious association and allows that most powerful part of your mind to stay focused on the ASM.

I have used this extraordinarily powerful technique with successful people to help them reach new levels of performance and achievement, and also with people to help them achieve very specific short-term goals. Such as finding a key member of staff who they needed to recruit to fill a key function in their growing business, finding and buying their dream home. Even having the car they always wanted but thought was impractical.

In that last instance, the Visual-is-ACTION involved them imagining they were walking up to the car, their car (specific colour, personal number plate and all), clicking the alarm button on the key fob, opening the door, getting into the car, the smell of the leather upholstery, and driving through country lanes with the roof down, sun shining, wind in their hair. You get the idea, I'm sure, and you can create similar Visual-is-ACTIONs for your own ASMs.

Chapter key points

■ You know where you want to get to, you know the route to take, so now it's time for the first steps. But let's not make this one long slog.

■ The key to climbing your 'mountain' is to focus on a few breakthroughs, sustained.

■ Begin by setting 1–3 ASMs: 90-day breakthrough goals that help you accelerate along the route.

■ Use the Star Card Visual-is-ACTION technique to keep your subconscious focused, too.

■ Then go all out to achieve these ASMs.

Action Zone
Time to download

My 'ASMs' Action Zone

What I have learned	What I am going to do about it

CHAPTER 9

Motiv-ACTION

*'He who has a "why" to live
Can bear almost any "how".'* NIETZSCHE

So far I have not talked explicitly about motivation, focusing instead on the power of mindset. You see, when your subconscious mindset is deployed to great effect, it's not a case of summoning up immense reserves of motivation in order to push you to greater heights. You soar to greater heights because of what you are thinking, believing and therefore doing at a subliminal level.

When it comes to achieving specific big breakthroughs, such as with your ASMs, it is important to apply some specific tools for motivation – to go the extra mile. However, it's not purely motivation in the traditional sense of just getting juiced up about a fresh new idea, and bubbling over with excitement. No, there are some very specific elements I have observed in the most successful people, about how they get motivated.

First up is the whole approach to the result to be achieved.

GOING FOR GOLD v. SETTLING FOR SILVER

This is about deciding to achieve the result. Yes, deciding. Not 'seeing if I can' or 'I'll try my best, but...' It's about certainty of commitment.

Imagine an athlete looking towards the Olympics, with the objective of winning Gold. Now, imagine the equivalent in your own field of endeavour, in your business, in your career. If you are going for Gold you need to be approaching this current year with a certain zest, a certain intensity and a certain mindset. A certain sense of purpose. A certain *focus*.

Are you? Or are you happy to settle for second best?

Test yourself on one of your own goals. Does it feel like going for Gold? Does it make you a little scared? Do you feel like saying, 'I must be MaD to be doing this'? Or is it very much in the same old *so-so* zone?

Settling for Silver is OK, as long as it's what you choose. It is, in fact, what most people do, even if they are not aware they are doing it. It still involves putting quite a lot into self-development, business and career growth. It can involve going on courses, seminars, training, reading the right books, and accessing the right material. And it can even involve putting a lot of new things into action, making some changes, taking some steps forward. That's great.

But don't kid yourself that you are going for Gold. In fact, to do so will lead only to frustration, because you feel you are 'doing many of the right things' – working really hard – but just reaching Silver all the time.

Doing a little bit better (or even quite a bit better) is no longer enough to warrant Gold. That's settling for Silver. Don't expect to get the Gold if your actions, and your approach, are those of someone who has settled for Silver.

The message is: going for Gold requires moving up to an extra level. By the way, it is *not* harder. In fact, in many ways it's easier. It just requires a different approach. A step change in expectation, desire, belief and commitment. Best part is, it's worth it.

You see, Motiv-ACTION is largely a case of making a decision. Once made, it's simply a case of honouring the promises you have made to yourself.

There will be adversity, and that's when your motivation gets tested – your reason for action comes under the spotlight. But you can break through that barrier, beat the test.

THE FEVER FORMULA

It is, at this point, appropriate to introduce the formula for making personal and business breakthroughs. You can apply this formula to each of your ASMs to ensure the best chance of achieving them, or in fact to any result you want to achieve.

F = Focus

E = Energy

V = Vision

E = Enthusiasm

R = Reason

Focus: beyond the goal/objective. In order to break through a target, you need to be focused beyond it. If you focus on hitting it, you may hit it, you may fall short, but you won't break through it.

Energy: include some very positively energised action as early and as urgently as possible to ensure a good start. Physical energy can help with the most basic business functions.

Vision: have a strong mental image of the completed task, in as much detail as possible. Literally see the successfully completed task in your mind's eye.

Enthusiasm: coupled with energy, in any undertaking this will engender speed and urgency. When you have energy and enthusiasm you can't help but get the job done in optimum time. Sometimes we need to *act* enthusiastic to generate real enthusiasm.

Reason: have a strong reason for doing the task. It must be a personal reason – and make you want to peak perform.

At my seminars I have often illustrated this point by creating a real breakthrough with a participant who gets to break through a wooden board (karate style) using this formula. The *focus* is at a point beyond the wood. The key skill is to make the required action with speed (not strength). *Energy* and *enthusiasm* do the trick here. Having a clear *vision* in mind of the board broken in two is crucial. The *reason* is created by peer-group pressure and support, and also by a very specific personal reason, which we create live.

On one occasion I was delivering a series of speaking seminars for an organisation to a group of business owners. At the first event, we finished off with the 'board-breaking' exercise, following the FEVER formula. The volunteer who came out to the front of the audience and broke the wooden board was due to take over the running of the business from his father in a few months. He was a fairly quiet fellow and, in fact, after the breakthrough, the event organiser said that it was perfect that he had volunteered, as it was exactly what he needed to give him more confidence.

At the next session three months later, the organiser came to me beforehand with an email from that volunteer from the previous event. The email told of the amazing transformation in himself and his business. He was now much more confident and had a new-found presence. His father had handed over much of the running of the business to him now, primarily as a result of his new-found personal power.

Most important was the fact that he had applied the FEVER formula, coupled with his own experience of having made that breakthrough with the lump of wood. On returning from the course, he had decided to double the sales target for the company. Many people thought it was 'impossible', of course – that he was 'mad'. But he had applied the breakthrough principles and, that day, three months on, he had achieved the target – a real ASM, achieved in just 90 days.

HAD TO'S

It's amazing to see people's performance transformed when they get a sense of 'having to' achieve a new level, a new result. You know, when you get a real motive, you'll find real resources you didn't know you had.

The example we always hear is that if you imagine you are standing on the roof of a tall building, hundreds of feet up in the sky. There's a plank, just six inches wide, bridging from this building, across to another tall building. Would you be prepared to walk across it? Probably not.

So, what happens if I say to you, 'You have to walk across', because on the other side a member of your family is being held at gunpoint and the kidnapper has agreed to some bizarre game in which he will release your loved one only if you make the traverse. Will you now walk the beam? I hope so.

The same motivation occurs in those people who are told they *have to* give up smoking or they will die. In fact, anyone would give up smoking if you held a gun to their head and said, 'If you smoke, I'll pull the trigger.' The key is having a powerful enough reason!

On a more 'normal' level, how many people have managed to lose all that weight they always wanted to lose because they want to fit into that wedding dress? Yes, there we have it, a sense of 'having to'. They want to walk down the aisle looking great, and can also imagine how terrible they might look if they don't lose the weight.

When setting your ASMs, always consider what you would be able to do if you really *had to*.

You see, these are no ordinary goals. We are setting them big and bold, and applying those same principles – a sense of *having to* achieve them.

So, what would you do if you *had to*:

- raise £1 million to pay the kidnappers of your children?
- run a marathon in six months' time?
- write your book in three months?
- give up smoking?
- get the business turnover doubled?
- launch that new product, service, website?
- redecorate that whole house, every room, in six weeks?

With your ASMs never say, 'I can't do it', without having first considered what you would do if you *had to*.

You will possibly be familiar with the scenario in which a lady is able to lift a two tonne vehicle off her injured trapped child following a car accident. This is the same level of Motiv-ACTION… it's a *'had to'* moment, isn't it?

And, by the way, you can play tricks with your *had to's*. For example, if you are riding a static bike in your gym, and you want to keep the speed above a certain level for a certain length of time, how about turning it into a scenario in your mind, crazy as it may seem, that you imagine, rather like in that well-known film, that you must keep the speed up or a bomb will explode, wiping you out. Consciously, you know it's just a little challenge you have set yourself. But, subconsciously, create the image of that scenario, and you will find reserves that will ramp up your performance. Try it, and you'll see, and feel the difference.

For example: action – to make an extra three key sales calls to potential clients today. Had to – imagine my life depended on making those calls. If I make the calls, I will diffuse the bomb under my seat. I absolutely have to, or boom – I will never see my family again.

When it comes to reason in the FEVER formula, always look for the 'personal dynamite' that ignites you to action. This will be related to your personal values, and to those things that give you pleasure in life. The reason has to feel like a reward and, often, the counter is a forfeit. So the achievement of the ASM gives a reward, beyond its own achievement. And failing to achieve the ASM brings a forfeit, in addition to not achieving the goal.

For example: if you set an ASM to achieve massive sales growth in the current quarter, or a huge number of new clients for your business, and you achieve it, the sales growth brings its own financial reward. But you must also provide an additional reward (typically people choose something like a weekend in a spa, or a trip to a London show, for example).

When it comes to setting the forfeit, this is where the fun starts! I remember one of my clients setting a reward of buying a wrist watch worth £1,000 for achieving a specific ASM. Great. I asked what his forfeit would be. 'Hmmm. Difficult one'. So, 'What's your least favourite political party?' I ventured. After he had answered, I then suggested he write a cheque that we would send to them as a donation if he failed to achieve his goal. He suggested £100. Of course, I upped the game considerably by saying that the cheque had to be £1,000, equivalent to the reward! I'm sure you can picture his reaction. And I'm sure you can imagine the levels of focus and commitment that went into the achievement of the ASM!

You see, we are making sure we play a very strong *motivation* card here.

Motive (reason) + ACTION = Motiv-ACTION

We are applying both pain and pleasure through the rewards and forfeits, to produce both a *pull* and a *push* to action. A carrot and a stick.

Chapter key points

- 'Going for Gold' in your results requires a certain approach to motivation.

- Motive-ACTION is about identifying, specifically, the level of commitment you are willing to invest.

- When reaching for greater results, apply the FEVER formula (Focus, Energy, Vision, Enthusiasm, Reason). In particular, create the reason for you to take dramatic action, as if you absolutely 'had to'.

Action Zone

Time to download

My 'Motiv-ACTION' Action Zone

What I have learned	What I am going to do about it

PART III

Go!
Action is the key

Focused action in a set direction to achieve a particular result aligned to a specific goal.

CHAPTER 10

Focused Action

'It's not enough to dream
It's not enough to try
It's not enough to set goals, or climb ladders.
It's not enough to value.
The effort has to be based on practical realities that
produce the result.' STEPHEN COVEY

MORE FROGS

Question: if there are three frogs sitting on a lily pad, and one decides to jump off, how many are left on the lily pad?

Two?

No.

There are still three. Because whilst one has *decided* to jump off, he hasn't done it yet.

> *Always remember that vision without action is just a pipe dream*

The action is key. Not necessarily complex action, or even a lot of action. Sometimes, simple, consistent action takes you there. But it must always be directed towards and focused on the result.

If, by now, you are itching to take action, great. The vision and the master plan you have created, your desire to deliver your unique talent to the world, and those clear awesome special missions you have set that create genuine breakthroughs, taking you 'up your mountain', will have filled you with a compulsion to get started.

So, let's make the action focused.

FOCUS

Focus is about bringing our whole attention to something – conscious and subconscious attention. It's about excluding any other distractions, too, so that full energy, time and action can be directed to the achievement of the result. So, we clearly need to decide the few actions that will create the results we want, to lead to the success we want. And we need to focus our attention on those actions. We need to 'put our mind to it'.

It is estimated that the human mind is able to focus consciously on between one and three things at a time. Whereas the subconscious processes millions of connections each second and is, in fact 'focusing' on much more information.

We all know what happens when you use a magnifying glass to direct the rays of the sun onto a piece of paper: the paper burns. That's because you have focused the heat and energy of the sun; enhanced its power. Like the sun, our subconscious is full of power. We need to show it where to shine, and that's what our goals (visions and ASMs) do. They act like the magnifying glass. And our actions flow from that power.

With the work we have done on the Visual-is-ACTION techniques, we have harnessed our subconscious focus. In fact, that doesn't feel like traditional focus at all. It's beyond focus. It's like an athlete going into the zone. It's freeing yourself to be brilliant.

Now it's time to turn to the specific conscious actions that lead to the results, too.

Attempts at 'balance' lead to trying to do too much, spreading yourself too thin. Having a laser focus on a few significant actions will lead to results more quickly than acting on many insignificant distractions. That seems obvious, doesn't it?

Yet, distractions are all around, creating displacement activity and dispersed focus. Many people like to wear the 'Busy-ness Badge' – they tell everyone they're busy because they think it confers some status – an implied level of success, and significance, a sense of self-importance: 'He must be successful, that's why he's so busy.' That's why they masquerade as 'busy' to impress. Because they tell everyone they are busy, they are easily seduced into distractions that lead to lots of activity: not productivity.

Focused action is not about taking any old action, but definite actions that lead to results. It's time to turn from being a 'workaholic' to a 'resultaholic'. You see, success is about putting energy and action in a set direction that leads to the result. It looks like 'busy'. But it's not, it's something far different. It's directed energy.

How many people have fallen for the multi-tasking myth? In my experience, multi-tasking means you are simply doing lots of things, below standard.

There's an important difference between being efficient, and being effective. Efficiency is all about *doing things right*. Effectiveness is about *doing the right things*. The key is to focus on effectiveness, rather than efficiency. In other words, we want to be:

> *DOING THE RIGHT THINGS*
> *BETTER*
> *rather than*
> *DOING LOTS OF THINGS RIGHT*

That's right. Focusing means doing fewer things! But what actions should you focus on?

THE KEY FACTOR

In every goal, in every awesome special mission, there is a critical element – the hook on which everything else hangs. The one result that will unlock the goal. Everything depends on this one element. I call it the key factor.

There are many other aspects that go towards achieving a goal, but standing head and shoulders above them is this key factor. Whether it's business or sales success, or personal goals, such as dieting and fitness.

To take some examples just to illustrate:

- In the case of marathon running, the *key factor* is running.
- For piano playing, yes, it's er, playing the piano, practising.
- In novel writing, it's the act of writing.

For business, the key factor may be less obvious. But it's still there – and I imagine you probably know what it is already, for each and every goal you are working on.

Looking at it from the outside, it is easy to identify a key factor. And yet, where many people fall down is in either not identifying their own key factors or, more often, in ignoring the *key factor*, normally because the key factor is that special ingredient that requires some harsh reality and consistent bold action.

If you want to discover what your *key factor* is, take a look at what it is that those people who are successful in a certain field *do*, and see if those who are unsuccessful also do it. Chances are that you will immediately spot the difference. The key factor is the *hard* thing that others just don't do, but which, if you can find a way of doing consistently well, will help you be world-class.

Success is about doing the things others just don't do – the things that:

Follow **O**ne **C**ause **U**ntil **S**uccessful

The key factor is where you get to show how committed to your results you are, to the goal, the vision. It's the opportunity to show your mental toughness, because this often boils down to the discipline of doing. With your key factor, the discipline of doing is always less painful than the regret of not doing!

The key factor, and whether you do it, is the test of whether you are truly serious about your success, and committed to your goal. It is a way of measuring the price you are willing to invest in success.

Doing what needs to be done creates success in its own right, it also creates belief in yourself that you are doing the right things and therefore are deserving of the success, thereby opening more doors and creating opportunities.

Not taking action also results in short-term guilt. And when our subconscious knows we should be doing things but we aren't doing them, it prevents us being 'successful'. Sometimes, because we are doing what we know we must do, we open doors and create coincidences that support us, often generating *luck*, which we didn't expect – things totally unrelated to the action, but that support us in the achievement of the goal. The golfer, Gary Player, famously said: 'Funny how, the harder I practise, the luckier I get.' So true.

Take this opportunity to decide what the key factor is for your own ASMs.

What one thing could you do that, if you did it consistently, would dramatically improve your results?

KEY RESULT AREAS (KRAs)

Success is about doing a few things well on a consistent basis. OK, we know our key factor – the one result leading to our success.

There will be a number of facets that contribute to the achievement of this. So, for example, for the salesperson to be successful, the key factor is making sales. Yes. And there are a number of activities that relate immediately to this.

- Prospecting for fresh clients.
- Arranging to meet them – making the calls.
- Conducting the meetings with them.
- Selling solutions for them.
- Following up.

This brings us to the 80/20 rule: or Pareto Principle, with which I am sure you are familiar. Briefly, Pareto was an Italian mathematician who observed in 1906 that 80 per cent of the land in Italy was owned by 20 per cent of the population; he developed the principle further and similar correlations were found with wealth and property in other areas of the world.

It is a common rule of thumb in business; e.g:

- 80 per cent of your sales come from 20 per cent of your clients.
- 80 per cent of your profits come from 20 per cent of your customers.
- 80 per cent of your sales are made by 20 per cent of your sales staff; and
- 20 per cent of your actions lead to 80 per cent of your results.

So, by focusing attention on those actions that have the greatest impact in leading to the results we want, we can improve our success.

The question, really, is do you know the 20 per cent of your actions that create 80 per cent of your results? And can you focus more on these actions, and reduce the amount of time, energy and focus applied to the actions that produce less?

In reality, there will be around five areas of activity that lead to your results: your key result areas (KRAs). This is about understanding the process of how you get your most important results, just as with the example of the salesperson earlier.

Being strong in these areas will achieve your results. Being weak in just one of these areas will jeopardise your results. And not investing the time, energy and focus into actions in these areas will mean you never achieve your results.

Many things may need to be done to support these KRAs, but focusing on them leads to success. And that means measuring: because what you can measure you can manage. You see, at each stage, for each KRA, those who are most successful set performance standards – quantity, quality, frequency, and so on. These are the yardstick by which you know you are taking focused action. They create a 'daily diet' of activity that revolves around your KRAs, that turns activity into productivity.

In addition, it's important to measure the performance and the actions, and equate these with the results you are getting, so that, in order to improve the results, you know where to make improvements in the actions (both in terms of quality and quantity). Once you know your numbers, you can plan to implement changes and have some knowledge of the results you will get.

It does require a slight change of focus from the norm. The key is to focus on the activity that produces the result, rather than on the result itself. That way you focus on the things you control – a system of productive actions. The results take care of themselves when you have a system of actions designed to lead to specific results. You see, focusing on results alone is very dangerous for consistency. Sometimes, results don't work out for you. But that mustn't impact your resolve to action. Most people are deflected from doing the right things because they are not getting instant results. So they stop taking the right actions that will lead to results. They also get disheartened because they were relying on results to fuel their mindset. You will notice that high achievers have a different focus – on the actions that lead to the results. They resolve to do the right things, better.

So, what KRAs does your success depend upon? What actions do you need to take? And what are the performance standards you set, daily/weekly/monthly?

When it comes to performance standards, it is important to develop habits that lead to the results we want, and we'll talk about building habits later on. The fact is, successful people have developed successful habits in their key result areas.

PERSISTENT PROGRESSION

The Hare and the Tortoise is one of the best-known of Aesop's Fables. We all know the story. Most people take one lesson from it: even a tortoise will win if it keeps going. Hmm. OK. That can be true. But we don't want to be just a 'plodder', and the story is about both the hare and the tortoise, not just the tortoise.

You see, I was always interested in the hare's part in the story, and the lessons to be learned. The hare was faster, got almost to the finish, got bored, ate some carrots and fell asleep… to be overtaken by the tortoise. So, the real lessons are not to do with the tortoise at all, other than to keep going. The lessons are more to do with the hare:

- Don't stop.

- Don't be complacent, or get bored with winning.

- Don't start reaping the rewards before the finish.

- Don't get distracted.

Don't eat fast food (hare fast food = carrots)... it sends you to sleep

Accepting that success is not a finishing line, but a journey, it's a journey of results, chosen or not, desired or not. We want to choose the desired results and that means taking action to achieve them.

One of the fundamental reasons people fail to achieve results is that they are unable to maintain their progress. The high achievers develop a progression in building their results, through consistent and persistent actions in a specific direction which builds towards a successful outcome. In too many cases, activity supplants productivity and, before you know it, you're just being 'busy' again.

Persistent progression is about taking direct action towards stated objectives. Being productive is also about quantifiable results, and that means measurement. You can see the progress, measure it, keep improving on it. This is PROGRESS-ion. When coupled with persistence, there's no more powerful force.

Persistent progression is akin to a ratchet. A ratchet is a device that allows continuous motion in only one direction. It normally has an arrangement of 'teeth' that allow movement forward and then act as a stopper to any backward movement. That's what persistent progression is about.

This principle applies when you take action. It's important to make that action a foundation for the next action, in order to grow, to progress. If you take the action once, but then slip back, you are starting all over again the next time. This is as true of business as it is of getting fit.

Think of this like 'crossing the gain line' in rugby parlance or, in American football, gaining your 10 yards. The idea is to have progressed beyond your previous position. It is going 'one step beyond' each time.

Successful people don't stop until a task is finished. They don't have lots of half-baked things lying around. They focus on a few things to the finish. And this applies no matter how repetitive a task seems. They simply keep going, till it's done. Sometimes, success is about not becoming bored with the progress. Many people want a quicker fix. They get bored with doing the 'hard yards' and are easily distracted. The regular action (even though it is genuine progress) becomes boring for them. Many give up, not because it was hard, but because they lost sight of the progress.

One of my personal clients, let's call him Jim, recently told me that he had decided to return to playing a musical instrument – an instrument that he hadn't picked up for four years. In fact, Jim had played this instrument for only three months (for about fifteen minutes, around four times per week). Then, like so many resolutions, it seemed to whither, for whatever reason.

The other day, when he resumed, Jim told me that he discovered two thoughts fleeting through his mind:

- Firstly, how amazed he was at how much he could remember and that, after a few minutes, he felt right back 'in the groove'.
- Secondly, he thought, 'How good I could have been now, if I had just kept on going with it over those intervening four years – just for 15 minutes every day.'

Isn't that like so many things in business, too? How much more business could you have got, just by doing the little things on a regular basis? Often it's the simple things that make the big difference. And success is often simple. But not easy!

In four years' time, what might you look back on and think, 'If only...'

BOLD ACTIONS

So far, we have talked about those actions that need to be consistent, those disciplines and habits that create results. There's another aspect of taking action that is clearly observable amongst high achievers: bold action.

This comes largely from the boldness of the visions they have set, the boldness of their master plan and of their ASMs, coupled with the 'step-up thinking' we covered earlier.

It results in injecting some quantum leaps at strategic points in the journey, and frequently. These are not short cuts, but leaps forward – leaps of faith and courage. It's about doing what others fail to do that puts you at the head of the success queue.

'Opportunities multiply as they are seized.' SUN TZU

CREATING BUTTERFLY MOMENTS

You know how, when faced with a big action that requires guts and some faith, you get that feeling in your stomach, some say like butterflies, but more akin to stampeding elephants!

If you can't remember the last time you had that sensation, it's highly probable you aren't challenging yourself enough. Because the sensation comes at that split second when you have made a bold decision, when the release of adrenalin hits you, and you are turning that decision into action. It is a sense of excitement as well as fear.

Many people associate it with the latter and quickly rescind or shrink back from the step forward. It's like being nine years old again, faced with a higher diving board at the swimming pool. You teeter on the edge and, if you take that plunge, the chances of you ever going back to a lower board are nil. But, even operating from the higher board never feels as good as the first time you harnessed that butterfly moment and stepped off.

Creating a butterfly moment is part and parcel of achieving results. If you aren't creating butterfly moments, you probably aren't taking the actions necessary to achieve the results that will lead to success. Seek out those moments and embrace them.

There's a subtle difference between the gut-feeling fear (knowing it's the right thing to do) and the alarm gut-feeling that it's the wrong thing to do. You will learn the difference only when using the Visual-is-ACTION techniques. In fact, when faced with a bold action, a butterfly moment, both responses initially seem the same. But deep down you know which it is. Act accordingly.

You know when you ask someone whether they have done something (such as a teenager and their homework), they will either say, 'Yes', when they have done it, or they will give a whole range of stories which mean 'no'? They don't say a flat, 'No'. It is the same with 'Have you finished that report?' 'Have you made that call?' 'Have you been to the gym today?'

The 'stories' also often occur in the moment just before an action is/isn't taken as a means of dismissing the potential actions.

The key here is to focus on the reasons to do, rather than the reasons not to do. You see, many people, even when they know they should be taking action, allow themselves to think of all the reasons not to do it, flooding their mind with difficulties, reasons why it's not the right time. Their mindset has a, 'Yes, but, no, but, yes, but, no' conversation – it goes into overdrive creating a series of stories to mask the inactivity.

In fact, they know the ridiculousness of not taking action. So, they create a 'logical' veneer, a multi-story mindset. These are excuses.

And in life, you are either *excusing* or *producing*.

We'll cover the whole subject of procrastination in the next chapter, but here it's important to understand the fundamental power of courage and the power of that gut-feeling that says, 'Just Do It!'

You see, when your subconscious is screaming at you to just get on with it, listen to it. Especially when you are doing the Visual-is-ACTION techniques we use in this book. The subconscious has a heightened awareness of what you want to achieve and sends you powerful messages to take actions that will lead to the success it sees.

In the same way that motivation and mindset are linked, so too courage and confidence are linked, but different. The exercising of courage (motivation), as a discipline at first, leads to confidence, as a habitual state of mind (mindset).

Exercise the courage muscle and it becomes stronger. Fail to exercise it and it will atrophy.

Courage needs to be summoned up, granted, especially when those butterfly moments strike. But that fluttering in the stomach is just life's way of testing your true commitment. It's asking you:

How serious are you about achieving the result?

'The World is moving so fast these days that the man who says it can't be done is generally interrupted by someone doing it!' HARRY EMERSON FOSDICK, AMERICAN CLERGYMAN

SITTING UNCOMFORTABLY?

When I'm out and about, I am a keen observer of human behaviour. On a recent train journey to Aberdeen, the carriage I was in was about half full. There was a mix of airline-style seats and double seats with tables (as we know, those are much sought-after!). Many of the airline seats were facing backwards – i.e. not in the direction of travel – and, like most people, I prefer to be facing forwards. To add to the discomfort of most passengers, the sun, being low in the sky at this time of year, was shining right into the carriage and most people were desperately trying to shield their eyes from the tortuous glare.

Then, at one station, a number of people got off, leaving several of the 'double seats' (four seats around a table) free. The train pulled away again. The next stop wasn't due for some time. But no one moved. No one got out of their uncomfortable position (facing the wrong way, with the sun in their eyes and with no space or a table to relax at). Interesting.

So, after a couple of minutes, I got up, smiled, moved the few paces across the aisle and sat down to enjoy the comfort of the rest of the journey, facing forward, able to read in comfort and do a bit of work. And I could tell that most of the other passengers were thinking: 'I wish I had done that.' Instead, they had got comfortable in their discomfort, and did nothing.

I'm sure you get the point. But have you noticed that you may be comfortable in your discomfort? Are you clinging onto the devil you know?

BEING A GREAT FINISHER

Successful achievers don't do more. But they do *finish* more. And what they finish, matters. It is significant and leads to a desired result, which, in turn, leads to a goal.

They also know the difference between perfect and polished. The former often stops people finishing because it can never be attained, and so they fall short of finishing. The latter is about finishing a task to your best ability. Finished.

One of the most sought-after qualities in business is the ability to finish. Being a great finisher will put you ahead of the competition in any field.

The first step is to realise what 'finished' means. We are not in search of perfection. We are in search of results. Not everything has to be perfect. We are aiming for a specific result. A polished result. But perfection is an unattainable myth. Define the specific result at the start of any task and have a 'no excuse' approach to taking the actions required to achieve it and you will finish.

Here's the good news: finishing is a habit. Like all habits, finishing can be learned. It's an invaluable skill. And, once you get into that habit, you'll be amazed at what you achieve.

Listening to a client, he talked about what his challenge is right now. He has so many opportunities to pursue, and so many things which are almost complete, but can't seem to get any of them done.

I suggested he took himself to 'finishing school' for a month.

Finishing school

It takes around 28 days to create a new habit (more of which later). So why not 'go to finishing school' for 28 days and learn how to be a finisher?

It doesn't just have to be about business, either. It could be around the home, in relation to personal life, anything really. The whole idea is to train yourself to be a finisher, to have the mindset of a finisher.

Lesson 1

Learn to decide what to finish. Are you having your time deflected to tasks that are not connected to your goals/objectives? Learn to focus only on those tasks that will lead you towards a goal or objective.

Lesson 2

Create a big list of all those things you can finish that will lead you forward. If they won't lead you forward, you need to decide to ditch them (and thereby finish them). Having unfinished stuff lying around is bad for your self-image/thought-print, so get rid of it, one way or another.

Lesson 3

Decide what 'finished' means in relation to these tasks. Note: it's about polished, not perfection.

Lesson 4

Apply the FEVER formula (Focus, Energy, Vision, Enthusiasm, Reason).

Lesson 5

Create the habit and mindset of a finisher.

This is where you get to take action: decide to finish something every day for 28 days. What you finish could be small or large. You could even decide which things you are going to finish on which day in advance.

Draw up a list of all the things you want to get finished over the next month. This includes all the half-started projects and little things which are hanging over. That could be business things from finishing a specific project to finishing a marketing flyer. It could be a report you have been putting off finishing, the preparations for a meeting or event that have dragged on too long, or that phone call that is overdue, or that meeting that really needs to be arranged. Or it could simply be that form that needs to be filled in.

Or they could be personal things (finishing the garden, finishing clearing out the cupboards, finishing putting all the photos in albums, finishing putting pictures up in the spare room, or painting the back bedroom and so on).

Once you have your list, invest an hour or two finishing one item every day. At work, set aside finishing time. At home, sacrifice the lazy TV time and just decide that between 8 and 9 pm (or whatever time suits) you are going to *finish* something.

Having a finishing binge like this will create fantastic results and opportunities and will also get you into the habit of being a finisher – a result-aholic!

Chapter key points

- Creating greater results is about taking action. Not just any old action, not just 'getting busy'. But focused action designed to create the results you want.

- Every goal rests on a key factor that unlocks the result. The successful achievement of this result depends on action taken in your Key Result Areas (there will be around five of these: what are yours?)

- To ensure you achieve results means persistence and progression through consistent action in these areas, coupled with taking bold 'butterfly in stomach' actions, and sometimes feeling a little uncomfortable.

- You can do it. And don't stop until you are finished. Too often people have too many unfinished tasks lying around. And too many results are lost by people who stop just before they achieve the goal.

Action Zone
Time to download

My 'Focused Action' Action Zone

What I have learned	What I am going to do about it

CHAPTER 11

Overcoming the Procrastination Pandemic

'Procrastination is one of the most common and deadliest of diseases and its toll on success and happiness is heavy.' WAYNE GRETZKY, CANADIAN ICE HOCKEY LEGEND

THE PROCRASTINATION PANDEMIC

Most people suffer from (or know a friend who suffers from) procrastination. In fact, I would go as far as to say that it's a virus of pandemic proportions – The Procrastination Pandemic.

Symptoms:

- **Wait increases**. An increase in 'Wait Watching'. Watching and waiting for something to happen.
- **Capability paralysis**. The belief that you can do everything. And because you can, you believe you should. This leads to overloading and grinding to a halt under a deluge of inconsequential *activity*.

- **Paralysis by analysis**. Thinking too hard about whether and when a task should be done.

- **Phone-ophobia – call reluctance**. Something many people suffer from in business. Picking up the phone is often far more effective than a screed by email.

- **Lack of direction**. Inability to work in a straight line. Likely to stumble around from one task to another, into anything that crops up; not knowing which way to turn.

- **Excessive listing**. Too many lists of things to do. Making the lists is a displacement for doing the work. If you list too much, you end up going round in circles.

- **Build up of static**. Loads of great ideas build up, but lack of energy means you are unable to move and you end up static.

- **Extreme should-dering**. Or 'shoulda'ing' as in I 'shoulda done this, I shoulda done that'.

- **Be a gonna**. In extreme cases (and most cases are): can cause you to be a gonna – 'one day I'm gonna do this', 'one day I'm gonna do that'. In the end, it's too late, you are a gone-r.

So, is there an antidote?

Well, the whole of this book is one big cure, I hope. Here are a few specific pills you can take:

- **Apply the Wifo rule: Worst in, first out**. Take one task that could be a bugbear for the day and tackle it first. This will free you from guilt for the rest of the day!

- **Make the first touch the *deciding* one**. This is the one-touch rule for paperwork. But note, I said the deciding touch – not necessarily the doing one – otherwise you may end up doing low-grade activities when something more important is needing attention. As you pick up the piece of paper, decide whether it is to be **F**iled away, **A**cted upon, **R**eferred to someone else, or **T**rashed.

  File

  Act

  Refer

  Trash

  .... on your paperwork. The same can work for emails, too.

- **Remember the 80/20 rule**. For example, when the task is to write a report, the 20 per cent of work at the start will get 80 per cent of the result, because it's often the thought of a big task that puts people off. Once the task has been scoped out and broken down into bite-sized chunks, it doesn't seem so bad. Then all you do is take the first small, easily achievable step.

- **Remember Motiv-ACTION** (see Chapter 9). Had to's ask, 'What if I *had* to do it?' You know, if it absolutely had to be done or you would face a firing squad. Set rewards – and forfeits. Apply the FEVER formula (**F** = Focus **E** – Energy **V** = Vision **E** = Enthusiasm **R** = Reason).

- **Eschew perfection**. Don't be paralysed into trying to be perfect. Yes, we want to excel and be brilliant, but not at the expense of something important not getting done for fear it won't be absolutely perfect. Perfection-hunting is often the death of a task.

And perfection is not just about the task itself, but about the timing. There's never a perfect time. You will never be ready if you wait. We tell ourselves we are 'getting ready for the right time' to justify not doing things.

The trouble for most people is that, in their mind, they are just putting things off – it's not a question of 'not doing', it's a question of not doing just yet – and, yet, that means they will never get done. We kid ourselves that we'll do it, eventually. So, here's the question to ask when facing a blocker, something you know you are putting off:

'If not now, when?'

Decide to put a specific date on when you will do it, if not now. Interestingly, there's very seldom a 'better' time. So doing it now is the best option. But this way you've made a definite choice to do it now.

- **Do it For Goodness Sake!** Sometimes, the hard-nosed coach within has to come to the fore and give you a bit of a talking to – in no uncertain terms. Something along the lines of: 'It's time to stop being a 'nearly person'. What are you afraid of? Don't die wondering. What's the hold up?' OK…

Let's get on with it

Remember, the discipline of doing is less painful than the regret of not.

'INTERFERENCE'

Procrastination has a rather unpleasant bedfellow, which I call interference. And by that I mean that nasty little voice in our heads that interferes with our ability to progress.

You know the one, it's very critical and it niggles away at your self-doubt: 'You've never been any good at that', 'You never stick to a diet, why bother starting', 'Your presentation is going to sound really boring', 'You're not really the type of person that gets promoted', and on and on it goes.

It prevents us taking action and, as such, it is the most fundamental barrier to us performing to our best and achieving results. It hampers businesses, teams and individuals. It's a nasty little virus in our 'neck-top' computer system and we need a healthy dose of antibiotics to get rid of it.

Interference Barrier Diagram 1

Interference comprises:

- **Self-doubt**. A niggling doubt in your own mind.
- **Self-sabotage**. Allowing other things to get in the way.
- **Self-fulfilling prophecies**. We predict for ourselves: 'I just knew that would happen!'
- **Success sabotage**. When you are on the verge of success you pull back from the brink.

- **Success resistance**. Because it means change and you'd rather stick with the devil you know.

The source of the interference – buzz and fuzz

Fuzz is the internal self-doubt, associations ('I've never been any good at…'). It is based on our own image of ourselves and what we can or can't do. It leads to self-sabotage – and creates self-fulfilling prophecies – 'That's just my luck, that is.'

Buzz is the external 'evidence' that we internalise. It is the stuff that seems to reinforce our own self-doubts and it is why we often misread the feedback we are getting from other people.

Someone questions what we are doing and we see it as a lack of confidence in our abilities, or they give us what we think is an 'odd' look and we think they are being critical of us. In either case, you have no idea what the other person is actually thinking, you are simply drawing the conclusion that fits with your view of the world.

Another example is when you say something bold, like: 'I'm going to have my best sales month ever' or 'I'm going to loose two stone by Christmas' and someone teases you by saying: 'Yeh, sure. We've heard that before! Been on one of those motivational seminars have we?!' And you think, 'Yes, I know. I've said it all before haven't I?! Well I'm going to do my best for a few days, and then it will all be forgotten until next time!' In fact, sometimes they don't even need to say anything – just one askance look, or a raise of the eyebrow and a curl of the lip, and you internalise that doubt.

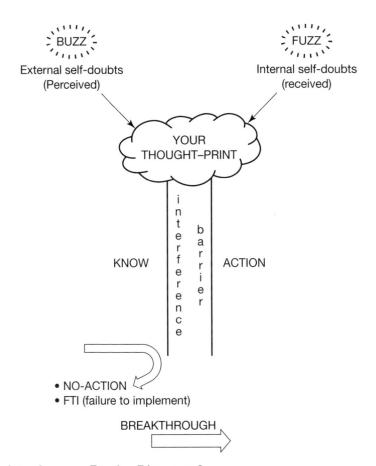

Interference Barrier Diagram 2

Interference leads to failure to implement (FTI)

Failure to implement (FTI) is the key reason people fail to make the desired improvements in any area of life – whether it is business-related, going on a diet, or an exercise regime – whatever the goal.

Most people have great intentions to make performance improvements. Many even attend training courses and seminars with high hopes of making changes. But returning to an in tray the size of a landfill site doesn't exactly help. And if the new ideas are not acted upon, they are very quickly forgotten.

Those who do get to the top have mastered the interference barrier and broken through it, and keep breaking through it once it starts up its useless chatter again. This allows them to consistently achieve better results, leading to greater success. They don't do it consciously – they aren't even aware they are handling it. They have a subconscious knack of overcoming it.

Remember when we talked about the achiever's mindset and how the associations we carry around in our head affect the way we behave (see Chapter 2)? They have a huge impact on our mindset. And so, in order to break through the interference barrier, it's with our mindset that we must begin.

Breaking through the 'interference' barrier is one of the most important keys to unlock your success, because it allows you to move swiftly from knowing what you can do to doing it, without interruption. And the real key to doing this is to create a new habit so you can jump the interference barrier as if it weren't there at all.

BANISHING PROCRASTINATION AND INTERFERENCE

For us to change our behaviours we must first change what we believe about ourselves – in our subconscious. That's why reprogramming our mindset is the key to overcoming procrastination and interference.

Once you can break through the psychological barriers, you will make many, almost imperceptible, changes and improvements in your actions, your words, your body language. This changes the way we see ourselves, the way others see us and, inevitably, our whole life.

Here's another Visual-is-ACTION technique to help establish this new more powerful mindset:

The Cards Visual-is-ACTION technique

Remember the key principles for our Visual-is-ACTIONs to work:

1 The mind cannot tell the difference between what is real and what is imagined.

2 Seeing is believing.

3 The images we carry around in our heads have a huge impact on the way we behave, on our performance and, therefore, on our results.

4 The subconscious is very child-like: very literal. What we feed in is believed.

5 What we feed into our subconscious controls our behaviours at a habitual level.

6 If we don't feed the subconscious in this way, it will seek other associations and make up an ad-hoc set of beliefs that will determine our behaviour.

So, here's how the Cards technique works.

The idea is to allow us to hold new beliefs about ourselves, and the way we perform, in all areas of our life so that we develop the mindset, actions and results consistent with the success we want.

So, take 20–30 changes/results/goals that you want to achieve for the next 12–15 months. These can be small things or large goals – they could be something like being more confident socially, to writing a novel, to getting fit, to doubling sales.

Write these out as a short phrase or sentence. Now write them in the past tense – as if the goals have already been achieved, or the changes have been made. For example: 'I feel so energetic and I look fantastic now that I am so much fitter.' This is much better than the mind carrying around the idea: 'I want to lose weight!'

Add some powerful language to the front, such as, 'Wow! It's brilliant how I feel so energetic and I look fantastic now that I am so much fitter.'

Then put each one onto an individual index card.

In each case, focus on the outcome, on the result of achieving the goal. Always state things in positive language, for example, 'gaining energy' is a much more powerful and positive image than 'losing weight'!

Use supercharged language – lots of powerful words, 'wow', 'fantastic', and so on, particularly at the front of the statement. This helps to gain the attention of the subconscious and also helps to move the focus to the result of achieving the goal, and how it will feel to have done it.

Once you have your 20–30 cards, take time out every day (I recommend first thing in the morning) and read the cards – word for word – every day. See and feel everything happening as if you have achieved what is on the cards. Don't just flick through them and think, 'Oh, that's my losing weight card', etc.

On one of the cards write: 'I am successful when I just get cracking and take massive action!'

After a few weeks you will notice many improvements being made, as will other people, and you will see results begin to happen.

In order to keep the cards fresh, you should add new ones and rewrite the old ones every four weeks.

I know that regular use of this Visual-is-ACTION technique will have a huge impact.

But a word of warning: I once met someone three weeks after they had attended one of my seminars – they said that they really liked the technique. I asked how they had got on with writing out the 20 cards. They explained that they really believed the technique would have a huge impact on their success, but they hadn't had time to buy the index cards yet, but, as soon as they could get chance to go to the stationery shop, they would get down to it.

I'm sure you get the message. The technique is amazingly powerful. If you use it.

HERE'S THE REAL SECRET TO SUCCESS

Ultimately, if you wish to turn your unique talent out into the world, if you want to achieve results that lead to success, you will need to put procrastination firmly behind you. Many people look for the 'secret' to success. They ignore the things that they think are 'common sense' or 'common knowledge', because they think success must be a secret path that no one else knows about.

But, in fact, it's seldom lack of knowledge of what to do that holds people back. It's lack of doing. Most people know how to get fitter, or how to get more sales in business, for example.

> *The trouble is that those things that are common sense and common knowledge are seldom common practice*

The route to success is not a secret one. In fact, it's a wide open path and you know your route to success very well indeed. You just need to walk down it and keep walking. If there is a secret, then it's a key; a key to unlock your potential and take that path. And the key is overcoming the interference barrier and allowing your common sense to become common practice by using your subconscious mind (which you access through the Visual-is-ACTION techniques).

Chapter key points

- One of the most common reasons people don't achieve results is procrastination. It has become a pandemic and, with our attention constantly being deflected, it is so easy to get distracted or end up stuck.

- Procrastination is a barrier between knowing what to do, and doing it. That barrier between knowing and action is in our minds. So, to break through it, use the Cards Visual-is-ACTION technique to create a new mindset – the mindset of an achiever.

Action Zone
Time to download

My 'Overcoming the Procrastination
Pandemic' Action Zone

What I have learned	What I am going to do about it

CHAPTER 12

Leveraging Resources

'Drive thy business, or it will drive thee.' BENJAMIN FRANKLIN

WHAT I LEARNED FROM A MEDITERRANEAN STREET ARTIST

It's early evening in the square amongst all the restaurants in a small Majorcan town, and an artist has come out to deliver his unique talent to the world.

The first evening I noticed him and something struck home – I'm always looking for examples of success principles at work. So, I decided to take a closer look the next evening. Getting a good seat in the restaurant nearby, I watched…

He set up the lighting, laid everything out and got thoroughly well-organised. Set out on the pavement were dozens of ready-prepared picture frames, spray cans (that's all he used) and a series of shapes to mask parts of the painting when applying the different coloured sprays.

His creations captured the island's atmosphere perfectly – vibrant colours, evocative of the Mediterranean tones all around us and, particularly, the sunsets, the sea, rocks and sand.

As he started to paint, a crowd gathered.

The artist was absolutely focused on his spray painting. Hardly acknowledging the crowd, he worked quickly and with great skill. He didn't take a moment's break, never removed the spray mask, and just kept on delivering his talent.

I observed how long each painting took and how many he sold. I was transfixed by the whole system. I'm sure everyone who went to that part of the island will have left with at least one of his paintings.

I also observed his assistant, interacting with customers, settling all the payment (not once did I see her struggle to have the right change), setting the paintings aside to dry, before carefully wrapping them up an hour later when the people returned to collect them.

The maths was astonishing. He painted around 10 to 12 per hour, and sold many more than that from his stock of pre-painted smaller versions. At 20–30 Euros each they made great presents and souvenirs. His four to five hours per evening were certainly well worth it.

Simplicity. Organisation. Delivering talent to the world. A study in time and energy effectiveness.

Leveraging resources is all about identifying:

- What you do well.
- Who you do it best for.
- How you can do it even better.
- How you can deliver it to the world, as effortlessly as possible.

And, for you as an individual, a team leader, a sales person, a business owner, whatever the size of organisation you work for:

> *Optimising resources is crucial for attaining results*

The combined effect of using your resources in tandem is magical to behold. It has a cumulative effect on your actions that leads to the achievement of results, in a similar way that compound interest builds money. Combining your resources, leveraging them effectively, creates exponential growth.

THE RESOURCE TRIANGLE

You see, fundamentally there are only three resources: time, energy, money. They can be exchanged one for another, of course.

What I have noticed about high achievers, and the most successful people and teams, is the way they use those three resources and how they get them to interact in order to achieve results. There is rarely any wastage. Whereas the underachievers do tend to waste their resources, often spending more of them than those who succeed.

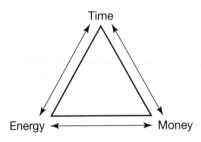

Resource Triangle

When it comes to your resources, there's a huge difference between spending and investing. Investing is about applying all three resources to optimum effect to achieve a result. It's a commitment.

Taking the triangle, those who succeed do so because they invest all three resources to achieve a result. They go 3/3. If they are not prepared to invest one of the resources, they go 0/3, and don't commit to the goal at all, instead moving to something else that they are committed to as a better use of resources.

Those who don't succeed tend to *spend* 1/3 or 2/3, and that's where the problems start, because you end up wasting the 1/3 or 2/3 you 'spend'.

So, when it comes to your goals, if committed 3/3 – do it. Or go for 0/3 – don't do it and move onto another, better opportunity or goal.

When I was a financial adviser, many years ago, I noticed that:

- 87 per cent of people spend all (or more than all) of the money coming into the household every month.
- 10 per cent save a small amount on deposit for the short term.
- 3 per cent make investments towards goals.

Again that's spending versus investing…

I bet the same is true for energy and time, if they could be measured in the same way. Most people fail to invest their resources, because they are not aware of the results they are aiming for. With no result in mind, people have a tendency to leak their resources. They end up spending too much money, rather than investing; expending energy rather than expanding it; and wasting time rather than committing it.

RESOURCE DRAINS

These days it seems to be regularly the case that half the UK spends half the year under threat of flood and then in the summer half of the UK has a water shortage. Then, inevitably, we hear about how the water companies are allowing huge amounts of water to be lost through leakage from pipes in need of repair.

To continue the analogy…

Imagine your resources are like water, flowing through your life carried by a network of pipes that ensure they reach those parts of your life that need them.

Well, if these water pipes leak, you need to repair them. If these pipes lead to a drain, where the water just flows away uselessly, you need to divert them to ensure they are feeding the parts of life that need them – the results we want to achieve.

So, where are the leaks in your resource system? What is it that drains your time, energy, money? What is it that you can change to make better use of your resources?

What is your number one resource drain?

And what leak-stopping measures have you put in place?

1 **Make a list of your top 1–3 resource drains**. Those that currently cause you to lose the greatest amount of profitable time or energy. You know what they are, I'm sure. And if you need a bit of help here the examples below will provoke ideas of your own. Don't be in denial over them. How can you regain the control, and stop the leak?

2 **Leak stopping**. next to each of your drains, write out a handling strategy, a set of boundaries and a set of ground rules that will stop the leakage. This is as much to do with awareness as with any neat trick which solves the issue.

Before we look at how this affects the business world and the way we perform, let me just illustrate more fully with an example from our everyday lives, and something many people would admit can be a huge resource drain.

One of the most common personal drains is TV... many people are in denial about how much time is wasted just sitting in front of the TV. The trick is to enjoy the TV you decide to watch, and not allow it to become your default activity. So here are some quick-fix tips to help reduce the leakage.

- Highlight the TV guide – at the beginning of the week highlight the programmes you want to watch that week and watch those only.

- Record programmes and watch them later, say at the weekend. Inevitably, you won't watch all that you have recorded.

- Never watch TV without having an alternative close at hand... that way TV becomes a genuine *option*, and not a lazy default. So, having a book at hand, or even a magazine article, a puzzle or a game as an alternative is a great way of taking control of the *choice*.

- Choose your programmes – enjoy them, and then enjoy using the *off* switch. Much of the drainage happens either side of the programmes we really want to watch. So avoid the overspill.

- If you are using the Star Card Visual-is-ACTION technique from earlier in relation to your ASMs, placing a gold star in the corner of the screen, and on the remote control, can have a great impact. How are you going to be a star, slumped in front of the TV? How are you going to achieve greatness just watching?

- Choose a hobby/interest/study/book/or whatever alternative you will do for 30 minutes a night. Fill the gap in your viewing with something productive and positive.

By employing this leak-stopping technique, we can soon create 'extra' time and, indeed, leverage all our resources.

It's simple to apply this same leak-stopping principle to your business life, too. Most people are frustrated by the same resource drains in business. Whether it is overlong/ill-prepared/ill-followed up meetings, an inability to overcome procrastination, poor delegation, or constant telephone interruptions. Don't be too busy to stop the leaks. Create handling strategies to ensure your resources are well invested in the areas that create results and lead to your success.

Meetings 46/60

The most common complaint I hear from business people is the ineffectiveness of the meetings they have, let alone the sheer volume of them. Having your people sitting at an ineffective meeting is a terrible waste of resources. Yet, meetings could be a means of galvanising resources, getting commitment to action. Now, you will no doubt have read hundreds of ideas in dozens of books on how to make meetings more effective. Here is just one idea:

**Why do most meetings default to an hour?
Because we use diary systems that are based on that!**

OK, if they have to last an hour, consider this:

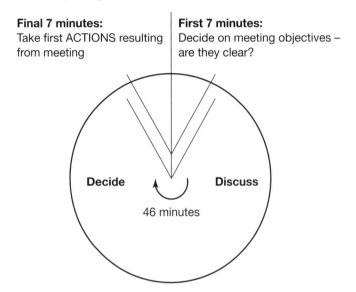

Final 7 minutes:
Take first ACTIONS resulting
from meeting

First 7 minutes:
Decide on meeting objectives –
are they clear?

Decide   **Discuss**

46 minutes

Meetings 46/60

This provides a better focus for your resources, in terms of time, energy and investment, and focuses on generating action.

Social networking or anti-social not-working

Let's take another simple example: the use of social media. The revolution in social media has been hugely positive for many businesses, and provides an incredible marketing and networking opportunity for even the smallest companies, as well as for individuals working within larger organisations.

Yet, we all know how it can become a resource drain if not utilised appropriately. Ironically, in business it is often referred to as 'social networking' and yet, for many, it can be quite the opposite – 'anti-social not-working'. The most important thing to be aware of is, what you are doing and why. Is it adding value to your goals or not?

For example, when you are gossiping and chattering with friends, that's social not-working (albeit, 'social' is a relative term here).

By the way, I'm not saying social networking is good or bad, or passing any judgement on individual styles of social media usage. The key, as with any of your resources, is awareness.

> *If you are aware of the leakage,*
> *you can stop it*

Money

We are going to cover the resources of time and energy in more detail in separate chapters coming up. Although it is not in the realms of this text to go into detail on the use of your money resource, some observations and fundamental principles are important to establish.

Where money is concerned, to create your best results, to leverage your resources, it's important to have the right relationship with money. Money is a tool, allowing you to function in your unique talent, to reach your goals. It is not a goal in itself. It is a tool.

The most valuable lesson I ever learned about price

Picture the scene:

You need an important heart operation and you have the choice of two surgeons – one is based in Harley Street, performs the same operation dozens of times each year, has testimonials from hundreds of delighted clients, and charges £20,000; and the other is a member of the local amateur surgeons association (they meet at the back room of The Pig and Whistle on a Tuesday evening), has never done a heart operation in the past, but reckons he can turn his hand to it for £1,200. Which one would you choose?

OK, I hope you have chosen wisely. Of course you did.

First thing to notice – it's never *really* about price.

The way to get more of this resource is to be abundantly clear about your relationship with money. *Abundant* being the operative word. You see, this is about abundance. A belief that there is an endless supply of money and all you need to do is tap into your big share of it in order to deliver brilliance to the world. But the delivery of brilliance comes first. Money is not the aim, just a function and by-product of success. Just as they believe there's an abundance of money, high achievers also believe there's an abundance of their ability (anyone's ability) to earn it, to deserve it.

So, you have a choice between the scarcity mentality – I haven't got enough, there is not enough – to an abundance mentality – there is more than enough, and by delivering my strengths to the world I will deserve my share.

When faced with the 'cost' of something, ask:

Is this related to my goals? And if so, am I willing to *invest* in it?

If 'No', then don't spend it.

If 'Yes', then... If I am serious about my goals, what's stopping me?

Whether buying or selling products and services, here is a wise approach:

> *'It is unwise to pay too much, but it is worse to pay too little. When you pay too much, you lose a little money ... that is all. When you pay too little, you sometimes lose everything, because the thing you bought was incapable of doing the things it was bought to do. The common law of business balance prohibits paying a little and getting a lot... it cannot be done. If you deal with the lowest bidder, it is well to add something for the risk you run... and if you do that, you will have enough to pay for the something better.'* ATTRIBUTED TO JOHN RUSKIN

- At a personal level, most people's relationship with money is based on fear. Fear of not having enough. And their worries are often born of uncertainty. Most people don't know where they are financially, which means it's difficult for them to know how to use what they have, because they don't know what they have, and because they don't know what the impact will be of them utilising some of it.

- The uncertainty and fear results in putting their head in the sand. And that's not a strong financial strategy. The first step is to get sorted. Grasp the nettle, sit down and get organised, both with what you have, and with what you want it to do for you.

Chapter key points

- In challenging times people don't have time, energy or money, to 'spend' dealing with those who waste such resources. So, if you are the sort of person who turns up late for meetings, who doesn't do what they say they will do, who doesn't follow up on commitments, whose dis-organisation has an impact on others (they always have to accommodate your last-minute changes to arrange-ments), there's bad news.

- Leveraging your resources is about investing, wholly, and getting more as a result. It's about understanding how to maximise your resources, and trade them for others' resources too. It's about ensuring every ounce you put in creates a return. It's about giving yourself the capacity to deliver more, to do more of what you are great at, to serve more, to deserve more, to give more to receive more. Yes, to earn more, to enjoy more, to *be* more.

Action Zone
Time to download

My 'Leveraging Resources' Action Zone

What I have learned	What I am going to do about it

CHAPTER 13

Time for Action

STRUCTURE

'I must govern the clock, not be governed by it.' GOLDA
MEIR, TEACHER AND POLITICIAN, FIRST FEMALE PRIME
MINISTER OF ISRAEL

> *Time management is a myth.*
> *You can't manage time*

What you can manage is what you put into the time you have.
This is as much about focusing on the actions that lead to the
results you want as it is about 'management' of time.

Think of a suspension bridge. At key intervals there are
major supports, interspersed with smaller struts all the way
across. Again, spacing of these supports is important. Too
far apart and the bridge would not be safely supported with
sufficient strength. Too close together and the bridge would
be too brittle, not flexible enough to withstand high winds
and pressure.

That's the way to view your time planning – a simple structure to allow the resources we have to be focused on the achievement of the results we want. On our journey, we have to be able to take stock at key points, and yet not all the time, otherwise the day-to-day actions that lead to results would not get done.

Just as with our goal setting and our master plan, we go from the wider general context to the specific. So, from a year's perspective to monthly, weekly, and daily time planning. So, starting with an overview of the year, let's see how time is to be allocated.

THE YEAR PLANNER

I'm a great believer in visible time planning, as you'll see. So, although gadgetry can be useful and there's a place for electronic diary systems, I know that most people work best when they are most *aware* of their time allocation – in other words, when it's right in front of them, clearly laid out, not stuck away in the bowels of a computer. Wall-chart year planners, and hand-written daily action plans are definitely in. We'll come to the latter shorty, but let's begin with how to plan your year.

The best way to illustrate the whole concept of creating a time structure for the year is to consider how it works for someone who runs their own business and then apply the same principles to your particular situation.

For those readers who run their own business, I am sure you are aware of the concept of working *in* your business and working *on* your business, as brilliantly developed by the author Michael Gerber. Working *in* your business is doing the operational day-to-day work with working *on* being the strategic growth work.

I like to add another element: time *off*. That time for *you* when you recharge, creating the self-efficacy required to keep pace in the modern business world.

So we've got time *in*, *on*, and *off*.

Let's allocate this within our year planner, beginning with time *off* – allocate your holidays and 'down time'. Do this by colour coding. I use bright sunny yellow.

For those who run their own businesses, I recommend 12 weeks *off* (or at least with the *choice* to be '*off*'). Now, if that makes you recoil in shock, time for you to make some changes, perhaps.

But whether you take 2 weeks or 12, the most fundamental point here is to recognise that when you are off you are *off*. Completely. This means no phone, no email, no twitter, no worrying about what's happening at the office.

Take this time to fully switch off from work, rather than wasting it in some sort of so-so middle ground of not quite working and not quite relaxing. I promise you that investing this time in being fully *off* will reap big benefits and you will return to work reinvigorated and ready to focus on getting results when you are working *on/in* the business.

Moving to time *on*, this is split into two different activities:

1 Hotel days. These should happen quarterly; they don't have to be in a hotel, but they do have to be a whole day away from the distractions of the office. These are the days where you work on the blueprint for your success, set fresh goals, identify the right opportunities to pursue and check in that you are still following the best path.

2 Monthly planning days (MPDs). Obviously these happen monthly – choose a day every month – the first Monday or last Friday, whatever works for you. These meetings enable you to check progress against the plan. They are for assessing sales, allocating finances and analysing performance; for uncovering any barriers, hiccups or challenges and deciding where you are aiming to be by the next monthly meeting.

For both of these you obviously need a clear agenda so that you can focus on achieving the most you can within the time you have.

There are other times for working *on* the business throughout the year, of course, but these are the main pillars in our suspension-bridge-style structure. For a business owner, every day should have some 'on' time allocated. This allows you to work continuously on improvements in business performance and results – always looking to improve, or to make decisive steps forward to specific goals.

Use colour coding on your wall chart: I use red for strategy – red circles for MPDs, and red triangles for hotel days.

There will be other days on which I have scheduled commitments, such as seminars and conventions, perhaps, or training, for example.

There are roughly 253 working days in the year. If you take 60 days *off* and invest 16 days *on* the business, there are 177 days left in which you can work *in* the business. These are the days when you work on your key result areas, able to fully focus on productivity. Now, if you are the business owner, that will also mean some '*on*' work, too.

It is sobering to look at the year and realise you have something like 180 actual days when you are 'over target', and then to work out your worth per hour based on your productivity target. It creates a better sense of urgency than thinking you have a whole year to do it.

Colour coding is important because it shows the gaps and balance – remember our suspension-bridge analogy. On one occasion a client was unsure how this could work for them, until they noticed, purely by observing the colour coding, how they had a huge gap between the start of the year and the Easter holidays (particularly late that year) and that then they had a lot of 'yellow' time until mid-August, then a huge gap till Christmas. The realisation dawned that this was a weak structure.

Remember, this is merely a template. I appreciate this whole system needs to be adapted to your own role and circumstances. But that is very easily done. Stick with the suspension-bridge principle, and a visual colour-coded wall planner and you will notice the difference. Remember also that this is a structure. And, just like a suspension bridge, it needs to be flexible. You will find times when things need to be switched around. Having the structure in the first place means that making such switches will not bring your self-organisation and time planning crashing into chaos.

WEEKLY TIME PLANNING

Most people find it easy to be focused once they have got focused. In other words, once we are performing well, we should keep going. Yet, in business, most people's days are disjointed, full of interruptions, so that no one really gets to pay the attention they want to the things that matter most, and many people feel they never really get going in such a way that they are performing at a peak.

I firmly believe that we are better to perform in *total* focus for three days per week, than to be in a sort of 'so-so zone' for five to six (or even seven) days. To be absolutely focused on your key result areas (KRAs) for three days per week, the other two days need to be used for admin, planning, strategy, self-development, reading and study, and so on.

Three steps to creating your outline weekly time plan are:

1 Identify your key result areas (see Chapter 10).
2 Identify all the rest of the things you do, and move them away from your focus days.
3 Create a solid weekly structure (again, not a straitjacket).

This should leave you with a week that could look something like this:

- Monday: self-development, creativity, reading and study, professional development, opening up and developing fresh opportunities.

- Tuesday–Thursday: focus days (reserved for KRA work and absolute focus).

- Friday: finishing up, admin and planning (including a self-organisation session).

Of course, the caveat rests that this needs to be a schedule that suits your role and work style.

The plain advantage of doing it this way is that anything that is likely to distract you from your KRAs is taken out of the focus days and put into a pigeon hole at an appropriate part of the week. So a 'valuable and interesting article' is put into the reading and study slot, rather than taking up focus time.

Self-organisation session (SOS)

An SOS because it's a real help – I recommend once per week you set aside time for 'staying on top of things'. This prevents you feeling out of control and being distracted by that feeling. It may take only a couple of hours or, depending on your role, it may be a half day or more.

In outline it is:

- Time to finish up – bring to a conclusion all the actions of the week and any productivity goals achieved.

- Time to clear up – all correspondence, all filing, all items off the desk; even clear out your email inbox – I like to 'zero' mine by 3 pm on Friday.

- Time to review the week gone – what were the highlights? What was the best thing, the 'champagne moment'? What were the lessons?

- Time to prepare for the week ahead – what are the priorities for next week? What preparation can be done now?

… which brings us to…

The weekly stratagram

Getting yourself organised for the week ahead is not just about allocating time, but also knowing your weekly priorities.

The weekly stratagram presented here owes a lot to the work of Stephen Covey, who developed a concept of awareness with his time quadrants, and to other time effectiveness techniques, which I have amalgamated onto one easy-to-use tool that will enhance your focus in planning actions consistent with your priorities.

Covey's time quadrants provide us with a time awareness concept:

Imagine four quadrants as shown in the following diagram.

Time Quadrants Diagram 1

Quadrant 1	**Quadrant 2**
Urgent and important	Important but not urgent
Urgent but not important	Neither urgent nor important
Quadrant 3	**Quadrant 4**

Urgent: those things that are pressing upon us.

Important: those things that attach to our goals and objectives.

Those tasks that are urgent and important are referred to as Quadrant 1 activity, and so on. The secret is to focus on investing more time in Quadrant 2. Consider this the quadrant of 'fire prevention' rather than always dealing with crises. It's the quadrant of working *on* your business. On its own this is a fantastic way to become aware of the need to spend more time on the most important issues.

The weekly stratagram uses this concept to help create a plan. The quadrants are redrawn to reflect the amount of time and focus that should be invested in them.

Time Quadrants Diagram 2

Quadrant 1	Quadrant 2
Urgent and important	Important

Urgent		Neither
Quadrant 3		**Quadrant 4**

We can add some other concepts we have covered already in the book to make this an even more powerful tool. Thinking of the week ahead, write the various goals and tasks into the appropriate quadrants.

This identifies your points of focus for the week and those things that take priority over all else. I have found that for Quadrant 2 a small 'mindmap' is the most appropriate way of working.

Also take note of your key result areas, and set specific performance standards for these for the week. This is a perfect way to finish up one week and prepare for the next, which is why it works best on a Friday afternoon.

Then, when you have recharged over the weekend, walking in on Monday morning you are faced with a clear view of where your priorities rest.

You can at this stage ask the Monday Morning Question:

'What is the one thing I can achieve this week that has the most impact in moving me towards my goals?'

Weekly Stratagram

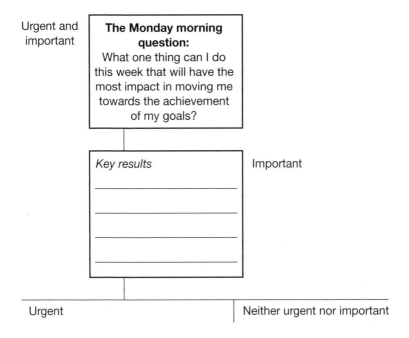

Having a strong plan for the week, with clear objectives and time slots, creates the context for daily time effectiveness.

DAILY TIME EFFECTIVENESS

Daily time planning on its own will not work. All it creates is a faster, more efficient (but not effective) hamster wheel. The context is so important, which is why it must be preceded by a clear vision, a master plan, a structured year plan and weekly priority planning.

Turning up

As Woody Allen said, '80 per cent of success is turning up.'

In the military, there's a saying: 'You must be in the right place, at the right time, in the right kit.' And, when it comes to 'turning up' each day, I don't just mean being there, but actually being in focused mode – with the right attitude: to the business of the day, to your colleagues, to your clients; committed to achieving results; with the focus on productivity, not just going through the motions.

By this stage in the text, you will need little explanation of this, and are in no doubt. In fact, I'm sure I am preaching to the converted here. Yet how often do people arrive at the office thinking, and sometimes saying, out loud, 'I hate Mondays', or 'I wish it was Friday'. Even in jest, such phrases trigger a whole mindset.

And let's switch on the necktop computer before we switch on the laptop. Yes, your most powerful gadget in your armoury. Time to engage the brain, and work out what is to be done for the day. The Visual-is-ACTION techniques certainly help: they create the mindset for achievement.

Realise the value of having the whole day stretching in front of you. Create this extra space at the start of the day to send a signal that you are in control. If you rush in and immediately fire up the inbox, you are straight into reactive mode. We want to be proactive, and our mindset must match that. So, once you have done your Visual-is-ACTIONs (I recommend at least doing the cards technique, the star card technique, and the lift technique every morning), take time to create your daily action plan.

Daily action plan

I once asked the CEO of a major business, 'If I had a magic wand for your company, what would you wish for?' He answered:

'I would start every day focused on a clear action plan for the day… and so would everyone in the organisation.'

There's a huge difference in approach if we use the term 'action plan' rather than 'to do lists'. With the former, you are being proactive. With the latter, you are a victim of a whole list of tasks. It feels like drudgery before you even start.

So, how can you construct a daily action plan?

First up, start the evening before. Just write out a list of items for the next day, taken from your weekly stratagram. Then, in the morning, it's time to convert the list into an action plan:

- It must be written.
- Use colour coding to identify your priorities.
- Identify the time-specific commitments in your diary.
- Identify the slots of time that are non-committed where you can place the priority tasks to be done.
- Ask a series of key questions:
  - What results do I want today, and what actions will take me there?

- What is the next bold step in achieving my ASMs?
- What are my three action goals for today?
- What must I finish?
- If I knew I couldn't fail, what bold action would I include on today's action plan? Why don't I just put that in today?

The time invested in this at the start of the day will reap huge dividends. You will be firmly focused on the actions that create results. And, if something 'crops up' during the day, it's a simple question of whether it takes priority or not. Again, it's more about time awareness than anything else.

> *'There are those who work all day,*
> *And there are those who dream all day,*
> *And there are those who invest an hour dreaming before setting to work to fulfil those dreams.*
> *Go into that third category, for there's practically no competition.'* STEVE ROSS, FOUNDER OF TIME WARNER

Golden hours

I was once coaching a business owner who said that, even though he wrote out a plan every day, he never got near the most important actions on his list. There was a mix of procrastination, but also frequent interruptions, and a lack of focus at play here.

I ventured that he should have a 'golden hour' every day. 'What's a golden hour?' he asked.

On average, business people are interrupted once every seven minutes – whether it is by a phone call, email, colleague, subordinate, or senior. It becomes a habit. And it's getting worse, with the buzzing of gadgets being a major source of interruption. So much so that many people self-sabotage and can't stay focused for more than seven minutes. The result is that, what would normally take an hour to do, now takes all day. And, conversely, we can get the day's most important work done in one hour, as long as we follow a few simple steps.

Imagine what it would be like to set aside an hour, free from interruptions, when you are able to get done those key actions that produce the most important results. As long as the time, and space and work, is organised in advance, it really is possible.

I call this the golden hour, and here are 10 keys to making it a success:

1   Put it in your diary – the most important hour of the day.

2   Focus on the end vision. Imagine how you will feel to have completed all of the key tasks, and the fantastic results they will produce for you.

3   Make sure you have plenty of physical energy available for this hour. It's no good booking it in for just after lunch.

4   Protect the time. Tell your secretary, PA and colleagues that you are not to be disturbed for the next hour.

5   Have someone take incoming messages for you. That way you can call them back in priority order. Not only is your golden hour extremely effective, but your next hour also because you have established control over the order in which you respond, based on *your* priorities.

6 Plan the hour in advance – have the relevant files available, the phone numbers prepared, and everything you need close at hand.

7 Work from a clear desk. Keep the one thing you are working on right in front of you, but nothing else. Don't allow your peripheral vision to be cluttered with other tasks.

8 Stay at your desk. Have all of the work set up in order on the right-hand side (preferably on a separate side table). Take one task at a time. When it's finished, move that file to the left-hand side (again a separate table, if possible).

9 Batch all your phone calls together. And know what you are going to say in advance. Have a single sheet on the front of each file with notes indicating the key points you need to discuss, or even a mindmap. That way, if you can't get through to the person, and they call you back later, the notes on the file will quickly remind you what you wanted to call about.

10 Once the golden hour is complete, reward yourself. You have probably completed the equivalent of one full day's work in a single hour. You've certainly done 80 per cent.

Start by having three such hours planned into your diary for the coming week. Then increase the pace over subsequent weeks. And watch the results flow.

> *Yesterday is a cancelled cheque.*
> *Tomorrow is a promissory note.*
> *Today is ready cash. Use it!*

Finishing up

Just as with 'turning up' each day, it's so important to finish up each day. Set 10 minutes aside to finish at the desk, take any final actions, and write the list for the next day. Note: if there are things on your plan for today that are not done, carry them forward to the next day, or beyond, if appropriate. If you have stayed focused on your priorities, they will be lower-grade items anyway, so don't beat yourself up over them.

This approach dramatically reduces stress because you are always working on your highest-priority items. If you achieve only three things, but they are your most important items that create results, that's far better than spending the day tackling low-priority tasks, even if they seem to be urgent. Resolve, every day, that, when you walk in tomorrow, you will have nothing of yesterday on your desk.

TIME TIPS AND GROUND RULES

Technological obesity: cut down on the techno-tyranny and get out of the gadget-mire!

Emails: do you really need that gadget bleeping all the time, creating a cacophony of distraction along with the tweeting and texts? I am amazed at how few people set aside email slots.

See how you get on with just three email-checking slots a day: 09:00; 12 noon; 16:30. Unless there are particular reasons for doing so (and I know some jobs do demand it – but certainly not all), why not try it for a week.

Do you really need to send an email and get into an email tennis match? How about picking up the phone and making a decision through speaking?

Copy-cat-itis: do you really need to copy so many people into this email? Stop clogging up the systems.

Twitter-time drainage: how about putting an egg timer next to your computer and, when you log onto tweet-deck (or whichever platform you use), turn the egg timer and stop when the timer does.

My simple number one ground rule on time is to be at all times:

- Working on your goals
- Working on yourself – growing
- Enjoying life: doing something for fun.

THE RICE BOWL

The Chinese have a phrase, 'Wu wei' – the power of natural action. Sometimes the power comes from the emptiness created by structure.

I once heard it described in relation to an analogy with a rice bowl. You see, a rice bowl's power is in its capacity to hold rice, and that comes from the empty centre. The rice bowl in itself has no value, other than through its emptiness – it is merely a structure. But without the bowl, the rice would simply fall on the ground and be lost.

Similarly, time effectiveness is about a structure. The true power, the capacity, is in what you put into the middle of this structure.

Some people like to 'go with the flow' when it comes to time planning. Yet, without a channel, there is no flow, just a flood. There's no need to over-plan. But there is a need to create a structure, a channel for your actions.

Chapter key points

- You can't do everything. The secret to being a result-aholic is to be fully focused at peak performance when it matters most – at chosen times on chosen actions which lead to chosen results.

- Creating a time structure that allows you to do this is at the heart of success.

- Whilst you can't 'manage time', you can create a structure that allows the optimum use of the time you have available.

- A simple structure must revolve around planning the allocation of time on a yearly, weekly and daily basis:

  – Year planner – allocating (strategic) on time; time off (to recharge and maintain self-efficacy); and time in, focused on your key result areas.

  – Weekly plan – identifying specific objectives for the week, laid out on a weekly Stratagram.

  – Daily action plan – a written plan, colour-coded to identify priorities, to ensure action every day is focused on achieving optimum results.

Action Zone

Time to download

My 'Time for Action' Action Zone

What I have learned	What I am going to do about it

CHAPTER 14

Energy

*'There is a vitality, a life force, an energy, a quickening
that is translated through you into action, and because
there is only one of you in all of time, this expression is
unique. And if you block it, it will never exist, and will be
lost.'* MARTHA GRAHAM, AMERICAN MODERN DANCER – THE
FIRST EVER TO PERFORM AT THE WHITE HOUSE

You will know many people who are high achievers and who
seem to have that boundless energy. They have a life-force,
vitality, personal zest. No, I'm not talking about just bags of
outward enthusiasm. There's more than that.

It's often mistaken for 'busy'. That's why people mimic
success by pretending to be busy, convincing themselves
(and others) that they are achieving results, being successful.
And they believe this will bring the same status.

In scientific terms, energy is defined as 'the capacity to do work'. Our chances of getting results, by taking action, will be impacted massively by our energy levels. As the world of business speeds up, so our energy demands increase. The laws of physics dictate that to double our speed we need to invest four times as much energy. In business terms, to achieve better results, where is this extra energy going to come from?

There are three ways to getting more energy:

1 **Make more**. Associate with positive people and do positive activities, have positive thoughts, use positive words and live/work in a positive environment. Energy begets energy: when we *invest* our energy, focusing it towards results that lead to our goals, the returns are positive, giving more energy.

2 **Waste less**. Don't be drained by low-grade activities, thoughts and people that are negative; less junk food and less junk TV also help.

3 **Maintaining high energy**. Through diet, fitness, rest and recuperation, and by having a structure that allows the flow of energy.

SLAYING THE ENERGY VAMPIRES

We all know those energy vampires, don't we – people in our place of work and in business who simply drain others.

They are, more often than not, very negative in attitude, have always got reasons why things cannot be done, and pour cold water on any new idea. Not only that, but they drain time, too, and hang around the darkest recesses of the workplace seeking a prey who will listen.

Slaying the energy vampires is essential in any team, organisation, business or, indeed, any walk of life, particularly in the current climate where working at full capacity is essential to achieving the highest possible results.

In the legends and movies, vampires are slain with a stake through the heart. Now, I'm not suggesting you do that to the moaning Minnie or whinging Walter at work, but here are some less extreme ways to slay the energy vampires you encounter:

S = Smile at them as they attempt to drain your energy.

T = Take control. Don't let them advance. 'Whilst I would love to carry on chatting…'

A = Appreciate their view, '… and I appreciate what you are saying…'

K = Knock it on the head. End the conversation, '… however, I am going to get on with x, so, if you'll excuse me.'

E = Exit, enthusiastically.

Remember, vampires can exist in many forms, so, not just in person, but online, over the phone, via email.

> ### Be on your guard

And, like any predator, they will always pick on the weakest prey. So make sure you keep your energy levels high. If the vampire is in your own head, like the 'sub-cranium demon' that keeps giving you negative thoughts (you know that voice that tells you that you can't do this or that, or you are no good at this or that, dwelling on past battles, blaming everyone from the CEO to the weather for all the ills of the world), release your inner champion to slay the beast – imagine your highest spirited attitude leaping into your mind like Buffy or Van Helsing and the vampire shrinking away, becoming a pile of dust, then a single speck and, finally, disappearing.

Chi Building: the Chinese have a wonderful term 'Chi', which means 'energy', but it's more than that. It's energy flow. And, when working on our goals, to achieve results, it's so important to ensure positive energy flow, especially within teams. A high level of respect and collaboration is required to allow individuals in a team to invest the extra energy required to achieve bold breakthroughs and big results.

Energy flow can be blocked or enhanced by the way we think because it reflects in our belief, commitment and behaviours when working towards a result. For example, a marketing campaign that a team had doubts about and weren't committed to will have less energy committed to it than the one that fully engaged and excited them, and the end result will follow suit. So, in order to achieve the biggest result, you need to ensure that you and your team have a high psychological buy-in and can release a burst of positive energy.

Similarly, the words we use are very powerful in generating an emotional connection to energy flow. Using emotive, dynamic words in relation to goals, particularly ASMs, gives more engagement with the result from the outset.

Remember from the FEVER formula (see Chapter 9): energy and enthusiasm = speed, urgency. This leads to bold action.

FIT FOR PURPOSE?

What do you see/feel about the person you are in your vision? Who is that person? Energetic? Fit, healthy, and confident? You bet!

We live in a shallow world and first impressions count. Not only the impression others have of us, but how we think of ourselves. How do you see yourself right now? Fit for purpose? This is crucial to what we believe about ourselves and our ability to achieve results. Interestingly, health and fitness is one of the most common reasons that people decide to take action at a personal level when I deliver business seminars, even when I hardly touch on the subject.

WEIGHT LOSS/ENERGY GAIN

Health is an issue. Let's not duck it. I have seen the effect it can have at both extremes: from those suffering from debilitating and, sometimes, sadly fatal illnesses through to people who operate at the highest levels of physical fitness and well-being. The contrast is stark. And, in the middle, the majority of us live; thinking that we really ought to do something about our fitness and general health, but putting it off for one excuse or another.

Well it's time to take personal resonsibility (TPR). Why? Well, on a few counts:

1 You increase your energy, ability to go for your goals, self-esteem and general well-being.

2 You reduce the risks of getting a serious illness.

3 If you are unlucky enough to get one, you increase the chances of surviving the illness and, in some cases, the treatment.

Perhaps the best way of describing how to lose weight is to recount my own experience of losing 28 lbs in 10 weeks. I wasn't hugely overweight, but, getting down from 14 stone to 12 stone, was an awesome special mission (ASM) I decided to take on in order to feel more energetic and look generally better, and all that I said earlier about ASMs, applies.

I should also add at this stage, I'm not a doctor, have no medical background, so all I can do is speak from experience. And I offer this, not as a specialist diet, only as a regime for 'normal' people. I'm not super-human, an athlete, just an average guy. So this can work for anyone who is in that same position.

First up: it's about changing your relationship with food. Recognise food as your fuel. The right foods give you energy. But many of us not only are not eating the right foods, but we are also indulging in foods that actually drain energy – high fat, high salt, high sugar foods that clog us up and slow us down. It's like putting 'leaded petrol' into an engine that's not designed for that.

> *Food is a tool to allow you to function. It's not an end in itself. It's a resource*

The mistake many people make is to focus on 'weight loss'. It is much better to think 'energy gain'.

My ground rules

- **Breakfast**: the most important meal of the day. Digestion is crucial, so why fill up with proteins or wheatgrain? Our bodies are designed (through millennia of evolution) to eat only fruit in the morning: think about it. That was what was available to primitive man. They didn't hunt till later in the day. So my ground-rule is to have nothing but fresh fruit juice before 12 noon. Buy yourself a juicer and use it daily.
- **Timing**: eat so you don't get hungry – every three hours.
- **Tea/coffee**: get off it. Drink water instead.
- **Eat nothing**: after 8.30 pm.

That was it. Simple ground rules.

Fitness and exercise

Again, I can speak only from experience, and I'm no Olympic athlete, I can tell you, but here's what I decided to do: I did some form of exercise for an hour per day. This enabled me to rapidly set a new habit for fitness. I started off gently by walking (not strolling, but really walking) and then stepped up to jogging/walking/jogging. Then running. It was simple and it worked.

Develop a weekly regime

It's important to set goals for weekly fitness and, of course the nature of these depends on your starting point. At a very basic level you might simply stick with the goal of exercising in some form for an hour every day. Or you might say to run three times per week is the goal. Or you might set performance targets as you get more proficient.

Here's mine:

- Monday: run
- Tuesday: powerwalk
- Wednesday: run
- Thursday: powerwalk
- Friday: leisurely long walk
- Saturday: longer run
- Sunday: free day

Regardless of assessing what's the best exercise programme, or the best way to exercise, it's about being active and having the exercise habit. So, every day is best, even if it is just for a powerwalk. There will be times when you simply can't fulfil the daily activity (these are rarer than you might think). Don't beat yourself up if you miss a day. Doing exercise regularly builds the habit, and you will resume the next day. Simple.

I have deliberately not talked here about gyms, weight training, swimming or cycling. I wanted to show you how you really can gain more energy with only a pair of trainers, not expensive gym memberships or equipment.

The rewards of such a regime

- Masses of energy.

- A sense of the new you, really having control over fuel intake.

- Hearing what others say. I still meet people I haven't seen for a few weeks and they are visibly taken aback, and positively gushing with compliments.

SELF-CARE

If you don't pay attention you can soon find your energy being sapped. So it's really important to look after yourself. You are, after all, your most important resource and, if you aren't firing on all cylinders, your chances of success are marginalised. Here are the basics:

- **Take time** *off*: this is to all you workaholics. You are actually damaging your chances of getting the results you want by relentless running round the wheel. If you really want to scale your success mountain, you must take breaks, recharge your batteries, refocus your mind and come back raring to go.

- **Get good quality sleep**: diet will help, breathing will help, and going to bed earlier will help.

- **Get up early**: this sends the signal that you want to be up, to be getting on with achieving results.

- **Eat well**: put good stuff into your body so it has the right fuel for maximum energy.

Energy mindset

Energy is an attitude of mind, as well as physical manifestation. So the images we carry around in our heads about how active, energetic and powerful we are reflect in our behaviours, actions and results.

Suggested Visual-is-ACTION cards to add to your pack

- 'Wow; it's fantastic how energetic I feel and how great I look. I feel amazing as people tell me how brilliant I look.'

- 'It's fantastic – every morning I am full of zest and energy and I love making every day the best I can. I have an exciting day ahead.'

- 'I love getting up early. It's great to start the day so positively.'

When working to a vision, and using our unique talent (doing what you love, at your best), psychological energy levels will automatically be high. We want to match that by ensuring we have the physical reserves to deliver peak performance and achieve best results. In the modern world, energy is going to become even more important to achieving results. Those who have it, in abundance, will win.

Chapter key points

- Energy is an invaluable resource for achieving results in today's fast-paced world. So, make sure you:
  - Build more
  - Waste less
  - And maintain your energy.

- 'Gaining energy' is a far more powerful mindset to have than 'trying to lose weight'.

- Make sure you are making choices that support you and give you optimum levels of energy.

Action Zone

Time to download

My 'Energy' Action Zone

What I have learned	What I am going to do about it

PART IV

And... Keep Going

Sustainability and consistency for true success

CHAPTER 15

Enabling Structures

'Be regular and orderly in your life so that you may be violent and original in your work.' GUSTAVE FLAUBERT, FRENCH WRITER AND NOVELIST

There is one further element to achieving lasting success. That's sustainability. And one of the most important aspects of sustainability is creating systems, which form enabling structures from within which you can operate at full peak performance capacity for extended periods – structures that enable you to perform your best work at your best.

Many people create results but soon get bogged down again and, just as we saw with the chapter on time effectiveness, it's often their systems that let them down. Frequently there's a recurring theme to what holds people back, and overcoming this requires a model solution, a structure that prevents the recurrence.

Developing enabling structures is about ensuring you are working on the most important activities, with your strengths and unique talent, by making the other essential activities as simple as possible to perform. So, it's often down to simple checklists, having a great team to help you, and delegating effectively.

There is not enough space here to develop the teamwork theme fully, and many great books have been written on that subject alone. However, the principles we have been covering throughout are equally applicable to a team.

When it comes to enabling structures, in essence, it's about having some very practical tools to help you flourish. Because it's your human brilliance that will achieve the results you want, I refer to this as systemise to humanise.

SYSTEMISE TO HUMANISE

One client, who I have coached for about a year, recently reported that he had written out a list of how his time had been allocated for two weeks. He discovered that 90 per cent of the things he was doing should be done by someone else (or not done at all). And I don't think he's alone.

For many people, the delegation bugbear is a difficulty, and the most frequent objection to delegating tasks is that, 'by the time I have trained someone and shown them how to do it, I may as well have done it myself!' Heard that before?

This is where having a robust system for 90 per cent (or more) of what you do allows you to delegate more easily, leaving you to focus your energies on the 10 per cent which will make the big difference to achieving the results you want.

In your own business, there are huge opportunities to adopt systems that are repeatable and that allow you to save 'mental hard-drive space' for the things that will make a difference. Many businesses, which grow to be amazingly successful, do so by adopting systems in a pyramid to support the primary function of the business. This is not about cluttering up the business with bureaucracy; it's about having structures in place so that you can perform the things that set you apart in a mind-blowing fashion.

Look for systems in your business and, whatever you are doing, ask, 'What's the system for this?'

Checklists and templates

Of all the tricks that I have learned over the last few years, this is one of the most important.

> *Work* in, *think* on

Let me explain.

Remember earlier we referred to the difference between working *on* the business and working *in* your business; working *on* your life or working *in* life? Working *on* is doing the strategic things that give you control and that help you to grow. Working *in* is the day-to-day operational stuff.

Of course, it's easier to say 'work *on* rather than *in*' than it is to actually do it. And, for many people, particularly those in the smallest businesses, the *in* work has to be done by them as well.

Yet, for every moment when you are working *in* the business, think 'how can I turn this into a system?' It makes so much sense to have a system for those things you are going to do regularly so that you don't allow your time and mind power to be constantly dealing with the routine stuff.

Let's take an example. If you regularly have meetings, do you have a checklist or template to prepare for these meetings? If you do, it gives you the time and energy to devote to how you are going to perform at these meetings, rather than spending your preparation time getting the routine things ready, and having to remember what those routine things are each time.

When I am going to speak at an event we have a checklist of all the props (magic wands, scorpions – yep! – caps and all the other paraphernalia) and all the materials I need to have packed in my case. That way, I can focus on what I am going to say, and how I am going to say it, rather than be thinking about whether or not I have remembered everything.

Sounds simple and obvious?

Sure it does. So how many checklists have you developed for the routine tasks in your business? And, when you do something for the first time, do you think *on* and say to yourself, 'What's the system here? How can I make this repeatable? What checklist do I need?'

Remember that over 90 per cent of the things you do are routine-based. If you systemise the 90 per cent, you can humanise the 10 per cent. And the advantages when you come to delegate these checklists to other people are enormous.

Devising a checklist for a task is almost like running a short training course for yourself. It's a way of examining your best practice. I now have a media interview checklist which is simply the 20 questions that I think they might ask. I practise answering them in as concise and clear a fashion as possible. It makes these things so much easier to approach.

So, what checklist could you develop today, which will mean that the next time you need to perform that task you can do it better?

ORDER AND ORGANISATION

Again, this is a recurring theme, of course, but I do hope you now see the value of being well-organised. It's no good being primed to commit to massive action to achieve stretching results in order to reach demanding goals, if you are going to get floored by being disorganised. And yet, we see it all too often.

As with planning and time effectiveness, the objective is not to be organised. The objective is to take action to achieve the results you want. That includes being well-organised so that you will be able to flourish, maintain focus and maximise your resources. For many people, being organised seems too much like hard work. And yet, if it's done properly at the outset, and maintained, it will give you a significant advantage, save you time and actually decrease your workload.

Remember the phrase: a place for everything, and everything in its place. This is not about being tidy. It's about freeing up time. You see, I know many people who spend hours looking for things, gathering together information, getting ready, sorting themselves out, time after time. They end up late for meetings, late with reports, late with phone calls, unprepared, and struggling to catch up with everyone else. And that has an impact on colleagues and clients. In fact, it has an impact way beyond just first impressions.

I once walked into a solicitor's office and was shocked at what I saw. My enduring image of this person is the heaps of files and paper on their desk, and an apparent lack of control. My thoughts: 'Do I really want this person to represent me? Are they going to know where my file is when I call them up with a question? Are they going to make a mistake that costs me? Are they even going to remember to return my calls?' I had no reason to doubt their technical legal skills, and yet... well, it wasn't necessarily going to be their technical legal skills that would win the day, get the result. I'm sure you see the point.

Creativity, and the capacity to deliver results, flourishes when your organisation allows it to. Imagine you are running a marathon and, within the first mile, you suddenly get that feeling that a small stone has got inside your running shoe. Do you continue to run, with that small jagged pain hampering your every step? Or do you stop, take off the shoe, shake out the pebble, put the shoe back on and continue running at full capacity? Of course, you do the latter. Otherwise you end up running the remaining 25 miles in pain, and at a lower level of performance. It takes only a matter of moments to remove the pebble. And yet, in business, in their lives in general, I see so many people who think they are 'too busy' to do the equivalent in terms of getting organised, of setting up enabling structures.

This is not about being organised for the sake of it. It's about being in control, free to function effortlessly and effectively, maintaining focus on the actions that create the results.

Spring clean

This may also mean having a clear out of all the clutter you have collected. Clear out your office, desk, bookshelves, home, loft, garage, shed and the cupboard under the stairs. Clear up anything that is hanging over from the past. A good 'spring clean' of your life is like sending a signal that you are ready to move forward and take advantage of new opportunities and create new results. The first person to receive that signal will be you – and that will make you feel rejuvenated.

In creating a clutter-free business and having nothing outstanding, you will often come across something to remind you of a business opportunity. Get up to date and you allow new opportunities to arrive. A signal to the 'business universe' that you are ready to receive, and that there is nothing in the way of you doing all the new business which will come your way.

This requires you to get decisive about all those things in your 'in tray' and the piles of paper on your desk, the emails in your inbox, and the odd files which seem to hide in briefcase compartments and get carried to and from the office every day, with all the good intentions of getting around to acting on them.

> *Clear your desk to the wood*

Upgrade your office environment

Now you are clutter-free, look at the environment you are in. Is your furniture really what it should be? Are you 'making do'? Are you well supported technologically?

Think about what your office space tells your clients, colleagues and bosses about you. These people want to be associated with success – is that what your space represents?

Again, the small things will make a huge difference here, and you don't have to spend a fortune to make the environment you work in very stylish, of high quality and supportive of your brand.

Just as a body finds it difficult to function with clogged arteries, and just as we feel re-energised when we spring clean, so, too, in our business and professional lives a 'spring clean' will yield immediate results.

Chapter key point

- Having enabling structures in place, being well-organised, clutter-free, gives you the capacity to do more of what you are great at, to achieve the results, to earn more, achieve more, give more – and, in turn, create more, be more, learn more. It's about organising yourself once and for all.

Action Zone

Time to download

My 'Enabling Structures' Action Zone

What I have learned	What I am going to do about it

CHAPTER 16

Having A Self-Upgrade

'Before you can do something, you must first be something.' GOETHE

To *become* the success, you have to first *be* the success.

We have talked a lot about changing beliefs in our subconscious mind. The visualisations we use are based on this and, to support that change in our subconscious belief, we need additional conscious 'evidence' that is congruous with the subconscious reprogramming you are doing. It's no good telling your subconscious one thing when all around you the evidence is pointing to something else.

Following on from the previous chapter, think of a successful business person who you don't know personally, but who you do know of. When I ask this at my seminars people often think of someone like Sir Richard Branson, for example.

Now imagine that successful business person in their office. Get that picture in your mind.

I bet the image most prominent in your mind is of that successful business person in a tidy, smart, clutter-free office. Right?

Yet, it doesn't matter whether Richard Branson's office is actually tidy (I have no idea whether it is, or isn't). What matters is your belief about successful people. You see, if the short-cut association you have in your mind is 'successful person, tidy office' and you walk into a shambles every morning, what is the message you are receiving, which is impacting your beliefs about your own level of success? Exactly.

And that brings us to the SP.

THE SP

Your **S**uccess **P**aradigm = your **S**tarting **P**oint.

A paradigm is simply a model view of the way the world works... and we all have paradigms through which we see the world. We all have a success paradigm (SP). This is a belief about what makes up a successful person. Often this will come from our observations of the behaviour of people we admire, our role models. Perhaps it will also be impacted by conversations we had when we were young, along the lines of, 'If you work hard and long hours, you too could one day own a car like that, son.' It's not surprising to find that many self-confessed 'workaholics' hold onto *this* particular paradigm. In essence, our SP is our subconscious model of a successful person's traits, behaviours, appearance/style and even a successful person's thoughts.

The images we hold in our heads about ourselves, our personal positioning in the world, have a huge impact on our behaviours, on the behaviours of others towards us, and on the relationships we build with the people around us.

> *Our outer world is a reflection of our inner world*

What we achieve on the outside mirrors what is going on inside, because our success in anything is first created within us.

Remember back to our discussion of our thought-print (see Chapter 2). The ability to build a strong inner vision is paramount.

The SP gap is the gap that exists between what you believe a successful person should be like (your success paradigm), and what you believe you are currently like (your starting position).

The SP gap is created if our inner vision doesn't match up with that model. And, for the vast majority of people, this is the case. Certainly, those with a strong self-image and inner vision do things very differently and it's the almost imperceptible little differences that combine to produce a powerful persona.

So how do we make sure our inner vision is unshakeable, powerful and positive? And how do we send those waves out to everyone we meet?

Mind the gap

Start by taking a blank sheet of A4 paper. Take a few moments to note down all those assumptions you have that make up your success paradigm. You might have things like:

- Successful people are well-organised and always work from a tidy desk.
- Successful people are fit and healthy and work out regularly.
- Successful people get up earlier.
- Successful people always look smartest in the room.
- And so on.

And don't leave anything out. This is most important. Don't think, 'That sounds silly, I'm not putting that down.' If it's there, record it. Sometimes it's the smallest things that make the biggest difference. At this stage, it's important simply to notice what your paradigm is.

So now you know what makes up your model of a successful person, the next step is to make up the gap.

And we do this by taking each element of your model and either ditching it or matching it.

Let's look at the 'ditching it' part first. Of course, very often, we hold things in our success paradigm which, upon examination, aren't true at all. Once we have identified these elements of our model, we can remove them from the model, and decide that they have no bearing on our success. This can, of course, be very difficult to do as some elements of our success paradigm will have been built up over many years.

It is really very difficult to change such deeply held beliefs with a fell swoop. Often it's much easier to simply 'match' the success paradigm.

In the case of matching it, take each aspect and set in place a regime to behave in a way that is consistent with the model.

Initially, you will probably have around 20 (or perhaps more) things on your list that can be tackled immediately. Many will be things that you can simply upgrade, such as the pen you use, for example (I know of at least one person whose paradigm was that successful people use an ink pen).

The fact that you are now matching your paradigm even in just a few areas will help you to feel and act more successfully. In turn, this will lead to more successful results, which makes it even easier to feel more successful, and so on. You are now on an upward spiral.

Does your behaviour match your results?

In order to create new results, and sustain them, we need to behave in a new way first. Not the other way round.

So, who is the person in your mind's eye when you wave the magic wand?

When you achieve great results in your mind's eye, who is that person?

Matching the success paradigm is about describing that version of you, and becoming that version of you. It's also about believing that you deserve to achieve the results you want because you are matching the paradigm, doing the things that are consistent with success.

SELF-UPGRADING

Let's take a structured approach to making this self-upgrade.

The way we think, the words we say, and the way we act, all have an impact on each other.

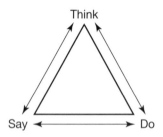

Self-upgrade Triangle

Think

> *'The ultimate freedom: the ability to choose one's attitude.'* VIKTOR FRANKL

Given that thoughts are things, then your attitude emits thoughts that rebound around the universe and cause certain effects. You tend to get back what you send out. In that way you have control over more than you think.

*What's happening in your
world is largely a reflection of
what's in your mind*

The first barrier you need to destroy is the constant junk feed that modern life throws at us. You really don't have to watch TV, read newspapers, or listen to crud radio. Yes, be fascinated by what's happening in the world, but don't allow external issues to bear down on you and drag you down.

Choosing your own attitude also means ignoring peer group rules for your success. These often begin at school where it is 'cool' to be unsuccessful. There's a culture, sadly particularly amongst young males, that says it is good to eschew achievement, in any form, perhaps with the exception of certain sports. The over-riding mindset created amongst the peer group, is to care very little about being any good at anything. This expands into later life where certain 'norms' are 'established' – 'I hate Mondays' and 'Thank God it's Friday' being two of the norms rolled out most often. Often accompanied by a sigh, these go hand in hand with a tut and a 'typical!' that heralds every piece of bad luck or any other barrier encountered during the day.

The message is clear: it's time to decide on your own rules for your success. Why not reverse the 'I hate Mondays' right now. Mondays are great because, after a refreshing weekend rest, they allow you to get on with the next stage in your journey, your true purpose in life. It's marvellous to start Mondays fully refreshed, relaxed, alert and feeling great. Make every Monday magical and marvellous. Why wouldn't you?

> *'No one can make me feel inferior without my consent.'*
> ELEANOR ROOSEVELT

Elastic banned

Choose one aspect of the way you think that you know is currently not helping you achieve results. It could be that you are fearful of something in particular, or 'dreading' a certain part of what you need to do to achieve a result.

Now, take an elastic band and put it on your wrist. When you feel that thinking coming into your head, snap the elastic band against your wrist. This is an awareness exercise. When you snap the elastic band, banish the old way of thinking and think in a new way, opposite to what you thought previously. So, for example, switch the thought to how much you are enjoying getting a result finished, and performing a particular part of that task. If you do this for around three to four days, you will notice how your thoughts change.

Say

The words you use have a huge impact on the way you think and the way you act and, consequently, on the results you achieve. For example, think of the difference between the word 'meeting' and the word 'appointment'.

Our psychological association is that an 'appointment' is where one person is doing something to another person (for example a doctor or dentist appointment). A 'meeting', on the other hand, is an exchange of equal value between two parties. Now, how many times in business do you hear people say, 'I have an appointment with...'? Better to think of such activities as 'meetings'. The way you subsequently approach that activity will be impacted by the word we use.

There are many more examples, and I'm sure you can think of a few. The fact is that changing the words you use and the way you use them (tone, volume, speed) has an impact on your results.

This also affects our communication with others and, in turn, affects the relationships we build.

> *The quality of your life is the quality of the relationships you have with yourself, with others, with the world around you*

Do

Imagine you are standing in front of an audience in three years' time. It's an audience of your peers, and you have been asked to speak to them about the secrets of your success and how you got to the top in your profession, your field. What are the three 'secrets to your success'?

Now make sure you are doing these things. These are a fundamental part of your success paradigm, so you may need to start acting it now.

'If you want to be the greatest company in the world, act it immediately.' TOM WATSON, IBM

This is the window on your mindset – and it's a two-way window. If you act enthusiastic, look enthusiastic, say things in a positive fashion, you will feel enthusiastic yourself and you will transmit this to others.

Sometimes, this acting needs to be put on. There are times when you might not quite feel 100 per cent. I won't pretend for one minute that anyone always feels 100 per cent. So, *act* enthusiastic and you will become it. But, most of the time, we can be more enthusiastic than we might be about life in general. As someone once said, 'Every day above ground is a great day!' Develop the habit of being 'on top of the world'.

> *You can't be the person you want to be tomorrow if you still feel like the person you were yesterday*

Change your actions in only a minor way and you change the results you are getting and, with the thousands of almost imperceptible actions, this creates a cumulative effect. And the cumulative effect of lots of new results creates major success, especially over the long term.

PROFESSIONAL UPGRADE

As well as the self-upgrading, there might be areas of your professional life that need upgrading: your knowledge, skills, levels of focused activity, and the structure of the way you go about your business. What needs to be upgraded immediately so it is consistent with the results you want to achieve?

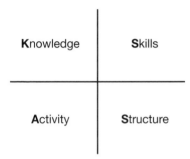

Knowledge   **Skills**

Activity   **Structure**

KSAS Diagram

Make this your professional improvement plan.

I once heard a company salesperson say that he was always too busy travelling to 'appointments' to spend time learning about his business, learning new skills, gaining more business knowledge.

I pointed out to him that his car was a mobile classroom and that, if he listened to just one audio programme on professional development, sales skills, or business improvement for an hour each day whilst driving, he would certainly raise his game. The light bulb went on! He immediately loaded up with materials and had his best sales quarter for three years.

BUSINESS UPGRADE

If you were a sports team, for example a football team, which division would you say you are in right now?

Most people tell me they imagine they are in the second tier, perhaps with a chance of promotion to the Premiership.

When I ask them what the criteria are for being promoted, I get numerous answers. In fact, in terms of English soccer, the two criteria for being promoted are:

- results – you must have the points total that puts you in a certain position in the league; and
- environment – you must have a stadium that is fit for the Premiership.

Interesting. When we judge our own business position, we often associate the environment with success. That's natural, of course.

So, in addition to the new results you want to achieve, what else needs to be upgraded in your business?

Can you set new standards, fresh ground rules in the way the business thinks (the team attitude, vision, atmosphere, approach), the way the business looks (its brand profile), the way you act in your business, the words you use (your marketing communication and words used within the team) and the business environment (clear out the clutter!)?

LOOK!

'Regardless of how you feel inside, always look like a winner. Even if you are behind, a sustained look of control and confidence can give you a mental edge that results in victory.' ARTHUR ASHE

Is your personal 'look' consistent with the results you want to achieve? Changing your look can have a huge impact on what you believe about yourself, the results you can achieve.

There's no getting away from it:

A polished professional look is essential

The number of salespeople who don't polish their shoes astounds me. I'm not expecting toe-caps like the Grenadier Guards, but the impression you create (particularly on the peripherals like shoes, pen, briefcase and jewellery) has a massive impact on the way you are perceived, by others, and in your own self-perception.

Visual-is-ACTION – the airship

Sit in a chair, comfortably, close your eyes. Relax.

Imagine you are in a hot-air balloon or airship. The balloon is secured by guy ropes to the ground. It is ready for lift off.

As you look out of the balloon, you are aware of someone on the ground close by who is smiling at you as you are taking in the scene. It is you. More accurately, you are aware it is the 'old you', the 'you' you are leaving behind, the 'you' with all the 'baggage', the lack of confidence, the negativity, the holding-back mentality.

The ropes are released and you start to rise, gradually. You are travelling upward away from the old you. You are leaving all that behind. You are waving goodbye to that person, and they are waving goodbye to you. You feel a weight lifting from your shoulders, and the airship taking you upwards. Allow the ascent to be about 20–30 seconds. All the while, the old you is disappearing from view, until they are out of sight, below the clouds.

You are now aware that you are starting to gradually descend. You are aware that you are bathed in a warm feeling and a beautiful colour all around you.

You approach the ground, feeling like the new you. You feel immersed in your own brilliance, totally energised, the new you – full of joy, professionalism, control, confidence. Feel totally confident, totally energised with personal power. Play this image through for around two to three minutes.

Now count back from 20 to 0. Slowly. Then, open your eyes.

You have landed.

Chapter key points

- Our results are greatly influenced by what we believe we can achieve. And what we believe is greatly influenced by the external evidence.

- To achieve greater results, and maintain them, it's crucial that the way you think, the words you use, the way you act, the way you look, and your environment, are all aligned with your 'success paradigm' – your model of success.

- Have a structured and deliberate upgrade both of yourself and your business/professional life in order to enhance your results.

Action Zone

Time to download

My 'Having A Self-Upgrade' Action Zone

What I have learned	What I am going to do about it

CHAPTER 17

Keeping On Track

'Always bear in mind that your own resolution to succeed is more important than any one thing.' ABRAHAM LINCOLN

For many people the challenge with continuing to get results is that they either get distracted or they get disheartened too easily.

This is where your mental toughness, your focus, your self-organisation and your belief in your goals will be tested. Doing what the majority fail to do puts you at the head of the success queue. The majority who don't *do*, don't succeed. The minority who *do*, succeed.

The modern world has made everyday living for most people increasingly convenient and easy. As a result, the traits we relied upon for our survival are starting to atrophy. Things like persistence, self-discipline, planning and organisation, decisiveness and a commitment to your goals. These are the things that also make up a checklist for success. These traits are all like muscles and will strengthen or atrophy depending on whether you use them or not.

The good news is that, if you maintain and strengthen them, your chances of creating results, of achieving success are much heightened.

There is no application form for success. But you have to *apply* yourself. And applying yourself to achieve the results you want is a matter of choice. You will be asked many questions along the way to test whether you stick with that choice. These questions will come in many guises.

BUILDING A JIGSAW

So let me ask you this:

If you had a jigsaw puzzle with all the pieces scattered out on the floor in front of you, and they were all blank, how difficult would it be to assemble the jigsaw?

Right. Very difficult.

Most of us are born with the all the pieces we need to build a successful life, some of us are lucky enough to have a sort of pattern on them and a few of the most successful will have begun to put the pieces in the right place. But many never experience the sudden dawning of the fact that it is they who have to decide on the pattern. All the pieces are there for you right now. You just have to decide to make your own pattern and put the puzzle together.

When making a jigsaw puzzle, you start by looking at the picture on the front of the box. It would be very difficult without this. That's your vision. You then gather all the pieces that form the edges of the picture, creating the outer framework. This is like laying the foundations of your success: the goals and the master plan.

You then turn to each of the key elements of the picture and decide which you are going to tackle first, gathering all the pieces that relate to that particular element, whether it's the cottage in the foreground, the sky, or the boat on the river. These elements are the awesome special missions (ASMs). And the act of putting the pieces together is the key factor – the action.

When my children were young, like many families, we made jigsaws. On one occasion, my son Christopher couldn't help being distracted by helping his younger sister, Victoria, to make her jigsaw too, leaning across and, in her mind, interfering. At the top of her voice Victoria shouted: 'Christopher! Stop making other people's jigsaws!' I remember the feeling distinctly as she told him off.

How many people in life get distracted from their own results, their own success, their own journey, interfering with other people's jigsaws?

Stop making other people's jigsaws!

Don't overwhelm yourself with other people's goals, issues and obstacles. There comes a point where staying on your own track is more valuable, not just to you but for the greater good, than being distracted. You are responsible for your own goals, your own results. Allow other people to be responsible for theirs, too.

THE YES/NO GAME

I'm sure we've all played the yes/no game. One person thinks of an item or a person, and the others ask questions to which the answers can be only yes/no, in order to derive clues so they can guess what the item is or who the person is.

The yes/no questions need to be very specific. Sometimes it can be difficult to give a yes/no answer.

In business, indeed in life in general, have you ever noticed that people find it easy to say 'yes' when they *are* achieving something, but, when they *aren't*, they tend to tell a story, to obfuscate, to start to explain away their actions (or inaction). I certainly notice it when coaching. So, instead of saying, 'No, I haven't done it', they will go round the houses and actually often change the subject to deflect onto something else.

So, when people are asked, 'Did you go to the gym twice this week?' they either say 'Yes,' or they say, 'Well, on Monday I had a meeting which went on longer than I thought, and then on Tuesday I was going to go, but I had to pick up some paper from the stationers first thing in the morning, and then Wednesday was a nightmare because someone had moved my waste-paper-bin...' and so on.

Yet, in the field of human endeavour, in the world of business, in any area of success, those who achieve most have a black/white attitude, a yes/no approach. They keep it simple. They also know whether they are 'producing' or 'excusing'.

The real breakthrough in achieving results is having absolute honesty with yourself and, when faced with a real challenge, realising that actually taking action is very often easier than the thought of doing so. In fact, you generate strength and momentum by doing it. Once you are started, it's easy to keep going. The discipline of starting is often all that's needed.

There are times, however, when genuine adversity strikes.

THE POWER OF ADVERSITY

I was watching the BBC Proms concerts on TV and, on one particular evening, it was Beethoven's Symphony No. 9 (the Choral). Some of you may be familiar with it. It is, in fact, a marvellous piece of music. Made more marvellous by the fact that Beethoven was totally deaf by the time he composed it. In fact, when it was premiered, he had to be tapped on the shoulder at the end so that he would turn round to see the tumultuous applause of the audience.

Watching the performance on TV got me thinking about success, about achievement, about what it is to create an extraordinary result.

I hear lots of people say things like, 'Well, I'll get onto doing something about that goal (or ASM) once I've got myself organised, once the children are older, once the weather gets better, after the football season finishes...' and so on. Something's always not quite right – either it's the wrong time, they're too busy, or it's the wrong market conditions, and they allow these things to prevent them getting on with achieving (or even, in some cases, starting).

And there are others who start out on the journey to a goal with great intentions, but, when faced with the first signs of adversity, they slip back into a more comfortable position and even deny that they had the goal in the first place.

So, what's this got to do with Beethoven's 9th/the power of adversity?

Beethoven didn't see his deafness as a weakness that prevented him carrying out his life's work in continuing to create masterpieces. And nor should we view the fact that conditions might not be perfect as a reason for not achieving results, living an extraordinarily successful life.

In fact, the achievement is made greater because of the adversity. It's only a goal worth achieving if there is adversity. Weakness, overcoming adversity, facing your greatest challenge is the goal. Your finest hour is heralded by adversity.

Look out for the flak

My uncle was a very young crewman in the RAF during the Second World War. He was involved in night bombing raids in the second half of the war. A terrifying and terrible experience, I am sure. Like many who went through it, he rarely spoke of it.

But, during those night raids, it was, of course, very difficult to navigate and apparently you only knew when you were near the target when you were under fire, enduring the flak from the anti-aircraft guns. The more intense the flak, the closer to the target you knew you were. That's right. The flak tells you that you are near the goal.

The message for us is clear.

Recognise adversity, as a test. Use it as a motivation. Turn it to advantage by seeing it as life testing your true commitment to your goals.

KEEPING YOUR FAITH

It's friction that polishes rough stones into gems.
It's the darkest hours that are just before the dawn.
When faced with genuine adversity, it is just part of the journey to success.
An obstacle is a signpost to what you need to do to achieve the goal.
That's all

'A lot of what we ascribe to luck is not luck at all.
It's seizing the day and accepting responsibility for your
* future.*
It's seeing what other people don't see,
And pursuing that vision.' HOWARD SCHULTZ, FOUNDER
OF STARBUCKS

Remember, Decca turned down the Beatles. And it is reputed that Walt Disney was turned down by 107 banks for a loan to set up Disney and J.K. Rowling was dismissed by many publishers before someone at Bloomsbury saw the possibilities in the story of a young wizard called Harry.

If you were watching a film and it began with the good guys winning, it wouldn't be much of a story, would it? The good guys have to start off in dire straits, so that we can all enjoy the comeback, the journey they take to victory. That's the nature of goals: they are goals only because they require you to overcome the challenge. No challenge, no goal, no success.

One of my clients contacted me to say they had had a real setback in their life's goal. They were upset, deflated, feeling generally 'yuk' about it.

This was the message for them, and for you if you ever suffer a setback:

- **Rebuild yourself**. Take time out to do so. Count your blessings, strengthen yourself.
- **Refresh your vision of the big goal**. Look long term again. Focus on the overall long-term goal. Make the vision bigger, brighter, bolder and even more compelling and exciting (and don't forget the reason).

- **Plan your strategy**. Reconfigure the route to your goal from the new position. Circumstances have changed, so you need to just re-establish your plan.

- **Simplify the actions** you need to take on a consistent and regular basis and write these down. Take action on the simplified steps to get there, now focusing just on these initial small steps.

STRUCTURES FOR SUSTAINABILITY

Weekly self-coaching

Monitoring progress and celebrating success is critical for anyone who wants to achieve their goals. Yet it is difficult to remain objective when doing this.

Self-coaching is the answer, and it is amazing the difference that a 30-minute session every week can make.

Here's what I suggest…

1 Set aside a specific time in your diary to hold your self-coaching session. (Friday afternoons work well.)

2 Sit in a different chair away from your normal work area.

3 Have an agenda (see the self-coaching sheet below).

4 Write down your reflections on the past seven days:

- The 'champagne moment'

- Highlights

- Results

- Lessons
- Points of focus for the coming week.

5 Be objective.

6 Finish on a high.

Weekly Self-Coaching Session

Champagne moment

 Best thing this week

Agenda
• Champagne moment
• ASMs progress
• 'Wins' and highlights
• This week's lessons
• Points of focus for coming week
• Coming weeks action plan (weekly stratagram)

'Wins' and highlights of the week
1
2
3
4
5
6

Lessons

Points of focus for the coming week

Weekly highlights and the success log

We tend to find it easy to see what hasn't gone well in a week. In fact, most people carry that baggage around with them constantly. So, to redress the balance and spin our thoughts and beliefs in the opposite direction, writing a journal, and doing a 'highlights email' create a positive spin.

Now, I don't mean that you simply look at the figures and see if they match where you want to be. Of course, you will be monitoring business performance in that way. Yet, it amazes me how few people keep any form of journal. Or even look back on a week and jot down what has been successful.

I encourage all my clients to send me a weekly email just highlighting their progress – just a few bullet points of what has been great about the week. Again, it could be anything: from winning new business, to finding new offices, to appearing on radio, to winning an award, to even just having a successful meeting, or a fun night out.

The reason I encourage this is to 'spin the mindset'! Our subconscious then starts to look for things to write in our next episode.

Whilst it is very simple, the effect is always very powerful. In fact, I take great delight in seeing the scales fall from people's eyes when they send me their first ever weekly highlights email at close of play on a Friday.

You can extend this idea to teams by introducing a success log: a hard-backed notebook where each person writes down one thing they have achieved in the week.

Doing something as simple as this can have a massive impact on the way you think you approach business and on the results you consequently achieve.

Chapter key points

- One of the reasons people do not sustain their results is that they get too easily deflected off track. Stay focused on your course, and your cause. Don't be deflected by other people's 'issues'.

- Sometimes, especially if you are a leader, or running your own business, the 'loneliness of command' can leave you vulnerable to the slings and arrows of adversity. People say they sometimes find it difficult to keep going when the going is tough. Learn to recognise adversity and use its positive power and, if you do get knocked off course, have a strategy for getting back on course.

- Build in regular self-coaching structures to support you on your journey.

Action Zone

Time to download

My 'Keeping on Track' Action Zone

What I have learned	What I am going to do about it

CHAPTER 18

Building Brilliant Habits

'We are what we repeatedly do.
Excellence then is not an act, but a habit.
Character is habitual action.' ARISTOTLE

Successful people have successful habits. Unsuccessful people are held back by their unsuccessful habits. We default to habits, by definition. Success is simple. Not easy, but simple. It's about making a few key decisions and then doing a few key things really well, on a consistent basis.

Many successful people find it difficult to put into words what they are doing that makes them successful. They don't see themselves as putting in any extra effort, or summoning up huge reserves of motivation, courage or energy. Indeed, most of them can't understand what makes people unsuccessful, why others don't 'just do it'.

In my experience, I have found that most people know what they should be doing to achieve better results. In fact, as we have seen throughout, knowing what to do is not the challenge at all. The main barrier is taking action consistently.

Psychologists tell us that the human mind gives in to change somewhere between 21 and 31 days. So we tend to form new habits in this sort of timescale. I have found that 28 days to form a new success habit is about right and suits our purposes perfectly.

So, here's a challenge.

First, choose a habit to develop. Then, set a reward for completing it in the 28 days. Make sure the reward is commensurate with the nature and scale of the challenge.

Now, we're going to monitor the habit.

THE HABIT BUILDER GRID

I've used this with people for anything from giving up cigars, to implementing marketing ideas, to writing books.

1	2	3	4	5	6	7
8	9	10	11	12	13	14
15	16	17	18	19	20	21
22	23	24	25	26	27	28

The Habit Builder Grid

Here's how it works. Every day when you complete the new habit, put a tick in the requisite box on the grid, *in pencil*. The aim is to get 28 consecutive days with ticks on the grid.

Now, if you miss a day on the habit, you rub out *all* the ticks and start again at day 1.

You can imagine the effect of this, I'm sure. You certainly don't want to miss a day by the time you get to day 21, or even day 12. So, you find your determination to stick with the habit increases past a certain point and, even though the habit discipline starts to get tough around the third week, it is counteracted by your extra motivation not to go back to the start!

Stay focused on the reward and embrace the challenge. Be determined to win your personal battle. It really is worth it.

The grid is about monitoring progress and, at the same time, creating a compelling and challenging reason to go on. Initially it's about using discipline but moving the focus towards habit. After all, the discipline of doing something is less painful than the regret of not having done it. Once the habit is formed, the need for discipline no longer exists – and what we initially thought was a difficulty has become easy to maintain.

> *Regrets are a terminal pain,*
> *Disciplines are a painful fix,*
> *Habits are a painless cure*

WHICH HABITS?

One way of choosing your new habits is to look at three specific categories:

- Stop
- Start
- Improve

A stop habit is where you want to stop doing something you know is currently holding you back or works against you, or a habit you want to kick. For example, giving up smoking, chocolate, crisps, snacking, complaining about the boss.

A start habit is where you take on something new every day. For example, starting a fitness regime or, in business, a new regime where you will make two extra calls to prospective new clients every day.

An improvement habit is where you are taking an existing good habit and making it better; or taking something you do quite often but that you know if you did it more consistently or more frequently it would have a marked positive impact on your success. For example, writing an action plan at the start of *every* day.

If you are setting out to change more than one habit at the same time (I would recommend an absolute maximum of six habits to change at any one time using this method), the key here is to spread your habits across the three categories, if possible. I know from experience that those people whose habits are all stop habits (stopping smoking, giving up snacks and chocolate and other such disciplines) can find the 28-day challenge a miserable experience – and that is far from the effect we want it to have, isn't it?

Having said that, all habits require some discipline at first. That is a good feeling. Harness the positive power of that challenge.

THE INNER CHAMPION VERSUS YOUR SUB-CRANIUM DEMON

The Visual-is-ACTION techniques we have covered in this text will also help build habits, when done every day as described (and I'll summarise the specific techniques to use daily in Chapter 19). In addition, there's a further technique that allows you to build strong habits.

Throughout the day we reach an infinite number of 'tipping points' – moments of thought/decision around which you act. They are often little decisions, almost imperceptible. For example, shall I write my book, or not; shall I mow the lawn or not, shall I get up and exercise or shall I just take a few more minutes listening to the radio from the cosiness of my bed; shall I do some 'urgent' admin or some sales calls instead? Even though these moments might be imperceptible, they are still a moment of decision.

At each tipping point there are a myriad number of possible courses to take. Each has myriad results leading to an infinite number of consequences and a new set of tipping points. So, it is impossible to consciously calculate all these options, outcomes and further options. We, therefore, default to our habits.

There are some moments of sheer brilliance. This is where your inner champion is at work. You know, those moments when you do make the positive choices which lead to success. You recognise these by the gut feeling you have of just having done something well. We've all seen the fantastic results of the inner champion's work.

Equally, there are times when the sub-cranium demon is at work. In the same way, your gut feeling tells you when you are letting him win. But he has a canny way of covering his tracks – he creates disguises and wears a mask. These are the 'excuses' we often come up with when we have allowed him to win.

He compounds this by also adding another sour aftertaste in the form of guilt. This guilt tells us we know we have let him win and, not only that, but he has the up on us and we are always going to succumb to him. He tells us he has won. And he also tells us we are weak, we are always going to be under his spell and that resistance is useless. These are all the ploys of our demon to help him win the next fight, to tip the scales in his favour at the next 'tipping point'. And he doesn't fight fair. He operates in a clandestine manner, and it's only once you have done his bidding/not done what you know you could have done (e.g. made that extra call) that you realise he has been at work at all.

We need to heighten our awareness of such 'tipping points' so that we allow the inner champion to shine and slay the sub-cranium demon. Enlarge the tipping points in your mind. Train the mind to recognise these moments and manufacture them so you can work them in your favour. Decide it's the inner champion who will prevail. Picture him, like a white paladin, rising up, with a flash of bright light and a swish of his blade slaying the demon.

> *Some of the time, we make the choices.*
> *But most of the time, it's the unmade choices that make us*

The easiest way to sustain new actions, to achieve greater results, is to make them habits, such that you no longer have to think about doing them, you no longer have to summon up extra reserves of motivation or 'step out of the comfort zone'. Of course, it's not a case of developing habits and then stopping. No, we become achievers only by continuous improvement.

We're slaves to our habits; we might as well make them good ones.

Chapter key points

- The most painless way to enhance performance is to make the new levels of action into habits.
- Successful people have successful habits. So which habits are supporting you, which are not, and which new habits do you need to build to step up a level?
- It takes approximately 28 days to build habits, so take up that challenge.

Action Zone
Time to download

My 'Building Brilliant Habits' Action Zone

What I have learned	What I am going to do about it

CHAPTER 19

Your Action Plan

So we've reached the end of the text... almost.

Hopefully, more than merely food for thought, there's a banquet of ideas that you are going to put into action.

Now, you have a choice...

You can

- **Do nothing**: stay where you are forever. Imagine what you will feel if you look back in 10 years' time and you had done nothing about improving your results.
- **Do a little**: perhaps, and slowly. OK, but remember what we have said about the speed of change in the modern world. Don't just end up treading water, or boiling in it, like the frog.
- **Engage fully**. Now. Get really serious about improving your results, with full-on commitment.

Yet, even if you choose the third option, you may be faced with an overwhelming array of all the ideas of what you could do.

I find it fascinating that people read books, go to business growth and personal effectiveness seminars and then, quick as a flash, they are back to doing what they always did. That's often because all the ideas are spinning round in their head, without any specific strategy for implementation. That is why I have included this chapter – a simple programme that you can set in motion within just a few days.

Of course, the changes you want to make are specific to your own circumstances. You might simply go back through the Action Zones at the end of each chapter and implement the ideas you have recorded, step by step.

The following is offered as a framework to follow to ensure you implement the crucial elements to allow you to achieve greater results in your business, career, and your life in general.

STEP-BY-STEP ACTION PLAN

Lay the foundations

Understand your values   See Chapters 1–5

Identify your unique talent   See Chapter 4

Identify your primary purpose and mission See Chapter 5

Create your vision   See Chapter 5

Create a master plan – The Mountain   See Chapter 6

- Identify your 'base camp'
- Identify the first steps on the mountain.

Get your act together

Clear out the clutter	See Chapter 15
Have a self-upgrade, business upgrade, professional upgrade	See Chapter 16
Have an energy upgrade	See Chapter 14
Create a time effectiveness structure: a year plan, including strategic time	See Chapter 13

Into action

Identify your ASMs for the next 90 days	See Chapter 8
Identify your key factor	See Chapter 10
Identify your KRAs	See Chapter 10
Create a weekly plan (weekly stratagram)	See Chapter 13
Create a daily action plan every day	See Chapter 13
Incorporate golden hours	See Chapter 13

Sustaining it

Remove the resource drains	See Chapter 12
Incorporate a weekly self-organisation session (SOS)	See Chapter 13
Introduce Brilliant Habits – take the 28 day challenge	See Chapter 18
Have a weekly self-coaching session	See Chapter 17
Use the Visual-is-ACTION toolkit	See below

THE Visual-is-ACTION TOOLKIT

Let me explain a little about how the Visual-is-ACTION techniques work best, and help you introduce a daily session that will dramatically influence your results.

First, allocate about 20 minutes for this at the start of the day, preferably immediately before writing your daily action plan. Now, I know what you are thinking, but it really is worth developing this as a habit. Switching on your necktop, remember.

Do not do this whilst driving. Find a quiet, comfortable place you can sit. Put on some headphones with some music that both relaxes and inspires you and that you can associate with success.

1 Your primary purpose: read this aloud   See Chapter 5

2 Your vision. This is a very simple
   engaging diagram of your vision   See Chapter 5

3 Image immersion technique   See below

4 The cards technique   See Chapter 11

5 The star card technique   See Chapter 8

6 The lift technique   See Chapter 5

7 Final two cards

   ■ 'I have made the decision to change.' See Chapter 1

   ■ 'I am fully responsible for everything
      I am, everything I have, and everything
      I become.'   See Chapter 3

The image immersion technique

Find several pictures (from magazines or online) of things relating to the results you want to achieve. These can be material items (such as car, house, boat, etc.), places you want to visit, or simply images that relate to a success you want to achieve (if you want to reach the position of receiving an award at your company conference or an industry award from your peers, a picture of an audience applauding you could be used). Make the picture about half a page of A4 in size. It's best to have between three and six of these pictures.

Each day, take one of the pictures (go with your gut-feeling as to which one you want to do – it doesn't have to be a regular pattern of one picture for Monday, then a different picture for Tuesday, and so on).

Hold the chosen picture about 12 inches away from your eye-line. Gaze at it, allowing yourself to relax into the image, and drift into it. Immerse yourself in it until you can imagine the picture wrapping round you and you are now sensing the whole event in the picture actually happening. Bring some action into the scene as you play it out in your mind's eye. See yourself achieving the result, feel the sense of success and personal achievement. Imagine what people are saying as they congratulate you, and what you are saying as you achieve it. Feel it happening, see it happening. Do this for around a minute.

THE EIGHT FOCUS PRINCIPLES

Remember, the key to getting results is FOCUS.

Here are the eight principles of focusing for results:

1 FOCUS on your unique talent – to do what you do best, at your best.

2 FOCUS on the brilliant execution in your key result areas.

3 FOCUS your resources of time, energy, money.

4 FOCUS on a few significant breakthroughs sustained.

5 FOCUS on the opportunities.

6 FOCUS on the extraordinary.

7 FOCUS on simplicity.

8 FOCUS on *purpose*.

Enthusi-ACTION: A REMINDER

At the beginning of this book I mentioned the concept of enthusi-ACTION.

Now it really comes into play.

It's often the case that we get enthusiastic about the changes we want to make, and the actions we want to take, and we allow that enthusiasm to bubble over and we even start to bore others by a constant reference to the changes we are going to make. They, in turn, give us an unhealthy dose of 'interference'. So, let's remove the talk, avoid the 'enthusiasm' and move straight to enthusi-ACTION. Let's take action and get some results, and allow others to see the difference first. Then you can allow them in on the secrets… but only after they have mentioned it first.

If you are using the techniques in this book, they will notice the changes, I promise.

And, more important than that, you will be getting the results.

Wishing you every success.

For regularly updated ideas on maintaining focus and achieving results, visit

www.philolley.com

where you will find complimentary downloads,

and access to The FOCUS Gym.

Like any muscle, our Focus strengthens with regular use.

The FOCUS Gym was founded by the author as a means to ensure you stay focused every day.

Designed for business owners, professional practitioners, sales people, team managers and strategic leaders, the gym takes the form of a regular daily broadcast by Phil, downloadable from the members' area, along with a number of easy-to-use templates to help you stay 'on top of the game' and achieve your best results.

The members' area also includes access to Phil's *Visual-is-ACTION techniques* as downloadable audio tracks, along with many more business growth strategies and personal effectiveness tools.

Index